Ferdinand Dennis and **Naseem Khan** have jointly edited *Voices of the Crossing*.

Ferdinand Dennis was a child-immigrant from Jamaica. His first book, *Behind the Frontlines: Journey into Afro-Britain*, was based on a journey through six English and Welsh cities and won the 1988 Martin Luther King Memorial Prize. Much of his work has explored the expressions of Africanness among African descendants. His most recent novel, *Duppy Conqueror*, was described by the *Guardian* as 'a landmark in British fiction'.

Naseem Khan co-edited *The Hustler*, one of the earliest Black community newspapers in the 1970s. She researched and wrote 'The Arts Britain Ignores' (1976), the report that heralded wide debate on diversity, the nature of British contemporary society and culture and helped to introduce a change in funding. She was the founding co-ordinator of MAAS, the national umbrella body for Black and Asian arts, has written regularly as a free-lance for the national press (including a weekly column for the *New Statesman* for three years in the 1980s on the arts, 'Work in Progress'), and is author of numerous reports – both as a previous Senior Associate of Comedia and independently – on arts and public policy. She was awarded an OBE in 1999 for 'services to cultural diversity'.

Voices of the Crossing

◆◆◆◆◆◆◆◆◆◆◆◆◆◆◆◆◆◆◆◆◆◆◆◆◆◆◆

*The impact of Britain on writers
from Asia, the Caribbean and Africa*

Edited by Ferdinand Dennis
and Naseem Khan

Funded by the ARTS COUNCIL OF ENGLAND

Library of Congress Catalog Card Number: 99–63336

A complete catalogue record for this book can be obtained
from the British Library on request

The right of the individual contributors to be acknowledged
as authors of their work has been asserted by them in accordance
with the Copyright, Designs and Patents Act 1988

Copyright © 2000 of the individual contributions remains
with the authors

Compilation copyright © 2000 Ferdinand Dennis and Naseem Khan

First published in 2000 by Serpent's Tail,
4 Blackstock Mews, London N4 2BT

website: www.serpentstail.com

Set in 10 pt Palatino by Intype London Ltd
Printed in Great Britain by Mackays of Chatham plc

10 9 8 7 6 5 4 3 2 1

Contents

❖❖❖❖❖❖❖❖❖❖❖❖❖

Preface
❖❖❖❖❖❖❖❖❖❖

Voices of the Crossing is an original collection of essays by –
mostly – British-based writers who started life in the Caribbean,
India and Africa. As editors we were interested in the features
of their backgrounds in those then British colonies – all now
independent nations and members of the Commonwealth – that
inspired them to write, and how the journey to, and residence
in, Britain impacted on them as writers.

The idea for this collection of essays was born in the early
nineties among a group of writers who recognised the very real
danger of the uniqueness of their contribution to English letters
being at best under-appreciated, at worst, lost. After several
unsuccessful efforts to find a willing publisher, James Berry – the
original progenitor of the project – entrusted it to us. Needless to
say, James Berry cannot be held responsible for any digression
from the original conception.

Several people have been of invaluable assistance in making
this book happen. Our thanks to Dr Alastair Niven who, as the
then director of literature at the Arts Council of England, agreed
to fund the project. A special thanks to Alastair also for collating
and editing Mulk Raj Anand's contribution into a single essay.
Stephen Greenberg was extremely helpful in facilitating the contribution from G. V. Desani. Thanks are also due to Gary
MacKeone, current director of literature at the Arts Council, and
Pete Ayrton of Serpent's Tail for their editorial advice, tireless
patience and cooperation. Finally, we would like to thank our
contributors for accepting and rising to the challenge of excava-
ting their memories with enthusiasm and panache.

FD
NK
1999

Introduction

❖❖❖❖❖❖❖❖❖❖❖❖❖❖❖❖❖❖

The fourteen writers of *Voices of the Crossing* are very disparate, yet together they form a coherent picture of the stages of the engagement between Britain and writers from its old colonies. They left their home countries at different stages in their lives and for different reasons, as long ago as the 1920s. The oldest of them is now in his eighties, and two – sadly – died before publication. The pieces printed here are Attia Hosain's and John Figueroa's last published work. Some of them are literary lions – G. V. Desani's extraordinary novel *All About H. Hatterr* preceded Rushdie in crafting an East–West oeuvre of surreal magic realism and was feted by literary London; John Figueroa was a stalwart of the impressive wave of Caribbean writers who emigrated from the 1940s and reshaped the language; Mulk Raj Anand's weighty novels introduced English readers to the Indian under-class and social issues. There are heroic women – Buchi Emecheta, Rukhsana Ahmad and Beryl Gilroy – who insisted ferociously on ploughing their own furrow, on building their lives as they wanted to.

But disparate as they all are, they share the same creative predicament – the fact of being located at a geographical, cultural and conceptual crossroads. The depth charge contained within that has, it could be argued, been responsible for releasing not only anxiety but also a distinctive creativity. And in each case that has been defined in a different way.

Many of them were aware, before their journey started, that the very act of crossing would bring them face to face with profound change. For many it was an extremely welcome prospect. The countries in which they had been born and raised were settled traditional cultures, compounded by the sterility of imperialism – oppressive for young men like James Berry who felt constrained by the poverty of lives that had been crippled by slavery; airless for young women like Rukhsana Ahmad, tied down in a tradition of powerlessness.

But for many, because of the patterns of colonialism, the divisions between cultures had already been fudged. The tentacles of Empire had taken hold of the middle classes and pulled them intellectually in different ways. Western images and concepts were the lingua franca of higher education (my own Indian father puzzled greatly, in his medical training, over textbook descriptions of bodily fluids having 'the appearance of pea soup'). The classics of Western literature formed the admired staple of a liberal colonial education. The ideas found in them were potent; they unlocked areas of the imagination that had been closed, and privileged the romantic idea of independent free choice in societies where the best wisdom had been to follow tradition. For some future writers – like Farrukh Dhondy, Dom Moraes and David Dabydeen – there was no place to be other than in the West. There they would find the publishers, the critics, the readers and the global markets. They slid relatively effortlessly into the limpid waters of Western literary life.

But the journey – as with all journeys – came with a price. Perhaps it was greater for writers from the Asian subcontinent than for those from the Caribbean: or at least radically different. For while all writers felt the effects – in different ways – of turning their backs on their own root cultures, for the Asian writers the question of language remained a problem. By choosing to write in English, they were immediately restricting their audiences (it has been estimated that 95 per cent on the Indian subcontinent do not read English), distancing themselves from vernacular writing and placing themselves in a very categorical space. It would be strange if they had taken that step without deep thought.

Rukhsana Ahmad and Attia Hosain are both eloquent in describing the nature of that dilemma: the attrition of the compromises, the torn and conflicting feelings that arose. For language, it goes without saying, is far more than an instrument to gain specific ends. It comes with its own history, roots, warmths and memory. Colonialism was of course keenly aware of the lifeline provided by language, which is why Africans shipped over to the United States and West Indies were deliberately mingled up, tribe by tribe, so that the common bond of language was broken. In colonial societies, the vernacular sank in status compared with English. It became the purlieu of the domestic, the personal, the powerless and the dispossessed. Buchi Emecheta retained hold of it however in the emphasis she placed on her own role as a storyteller, in the style of vernacular tale-spinners and history-carriers of West African society.

Turning away from the vernacular clearly induced deep and sharp feelings. While Dabydeen acknowledges that publication in England grants the validity a writer needs, he is also keenly aware of the limitations that using English imposes. The English language comes with its own terms: Dabydeen struggled, for instance, to describe the Guyanese topography in words that carried the romantic hinterland of the English country garden. Attia Hosain was constantly aware of what she had lost in using English. Her preferred subjects and her concepts belong to the lives of Urdu-speakers imbued in a certain kind of Muslim culture. It was impossible to translate those subtle courtesies directly without making them sound, to English ears, absurd.

The act of translation is a wider matter than words alone. All writers at the crossroads, without exception, are faced with the possibly unexpected task of having to define themselves. These writers fitted no known categories: they had sensibilities that had – because of their histories – become global ones. For the puzzled West, one answer for this phenomenon was to invent new pigeon holes. The writers themselves regarded the new labels with scant enthusiasm. Dabydeen rejected the term 'West Indian writer'. Ahmad rejects being an 'Asian female'. Ferdinand Dennis rejects the crude and simple power-lines implicit in the dual identities of 'Black' and 'White'.

The writers have all had to find their own locations, based in their own creative individuality, powered by a spirit that was fired by the inequities of racism. Some of the results have wild flights of imagination like Desani's *Hatterr* and – to a lesser degree of course – the piece printed here which was dictated after the state of Desani's eyes meant he could no longer write. Others have the warm observant humanity of James Berry's verse.

Homi Bhabha – a noted cultural theorist – puts it perhaps most elegantly. Coming to Britain with the vivid memories of the mish-mash kedgeree of Indian-British street culture, he had been repelled by the aridity of Oxbridge. His own base culture, he eventually concluded, had to be one that brought in all his contradictions and range: a 'vernacular cosmopolitanism'. It is this freewheeling personally driven culture that empowers its proponents: allows them to pick and choose, and to transcend old set boundaries of the mind.

The inner tension this involves and the regular choices it entails are clearly flagged up among the writers of *Voices of the Crossing*. In some cases, existing before their time, they took overt issue with the sharp lines between races and nations, past and present, arts and culture. Their lives have been lived in that uncomfortable location, the crossroads of culture. But the view they get from that vantage point and the despatches they send back give a longer view to the rest of us. They blur the lines of the map, subvert conventional categories and, in an ironic way, themselves colonise the unknown.

Naseem Khan

E. A. Markham

◆◆◆◆◆◆◆◆◆◆◆◆◆◆◆◆◆◆◆◆◆

Taking the Drawing Room Through Customs

E. A. Markham is a poet, playwright, novelist, and editor. As well as writing numerous original works, he has edited several anthologies of poetry and short stories. He is however best known as a poet who combines an elegant, precise style with profound observations on the human condition. In recent years, as Professor of Creative Writing, he has contributed to making Sheffield Hallam University's writing programme a huge success.

I'm hanging on to the old notebooks despite the chance to get rid of them; for the past year a university has been collecting my 'archival material'. So I feel that all these jottings of the past forty years properly belong in a corner of that institution's cellar. But I haven't finished with the stuff, the notes and stray entries waiting to be written up. I've just finished another box of – what? – work-in-progress, discarded versions and so on. It's of my latest collection of short stories, *Taking the Drawing Room Through Customs*. And even this box I'm unwilling to let go because the stories distilled from this raw material are only part of what I mean by 'taking the drawing room through customs'.

I see this particular drawing room, one I've been trying to make visible ever since we abandoned it in Montserrat in 1956 for England. Though there was no particular trauma in leaving it behind – we were quite looking forward to England – there was, on coming to England, some dismay to find the general assumption was that you had left nothing of value behind. Even fellow West Indians seemed to collude with this attitude. And trying to explain yourself was risky, for this was the context – student gatherings, nursing friends of my sister's, weekend dances and cricket matches – where people from overseas were seriously, if unconvincingly, engaged in rewriting their histories: so many young Africans claiming to be sons of chiefs didn't carry conviction.

In 1956, aged 16, I managed to avoid school for a couple of years, working in the rag trade, making ladies' belts and hand-bags and shoes in small workshops and factories in Baker Street, Great Portland Street and elsewhere in the West End of London. I was writing at the time and trying to teach myself languages. My eldest brother, Joe, used to take correspondence courses, so one lived in an environment of self-improvement. I mugged up on my Latin and Italian vocabulary while I put press studs in the belts and listened to Workers' Playtime on the radio, Ken Dodd and Gladys Morgan doing the jokes. Bad at languages, I assaulted the foreign vocabulary each afternoon when, with a bag full of freshly made belts, I set out to do the drop for my opposite number, Ivanov. But seriously . . .

Though I wrote a novel, mercifully lost, in the late 1950s, these were the heady days of theatre: *Look Back in Anger* (1956), Beckett, Ionesco & Co. Those of us trying to write dreamed of fulfilment on the stages of the Royal Court or at the Aldwych with Ken Tynan and Harold Hobson singing our praises in the *Observer* and the *Sunday Times*.

My playwriting debut was more modest. The first play pro-duced was at university in 1964. That was at Lampeter, where I was reading Philosophy and English. *The Masterpiece* was, in fact, a bit of a Platonic game, idealism coming up against the reality of the body. I'd had another play in rehearsal at BBC Radio in Cardiff, but that didn't materialise. In lieu of that, the putative director, Frank Davies, suggested that I apply for one of the BBC trainee producerships. But this seemed to someone of my arrogance a diversion from the real business of writing and I declined. Very much later I realised that some of my contemporaries, better briefed – Melvyn Bragg, David Frost – had taken up offers of BBC producerships. Towards the end of the sixties, I had the great good fortune to work with the theatre critic, John Elsom, both in writing and mounting group plays in the enormous front room of his house in Shepherd's Bush. My rejection slips from theatre managements over the past forty years are enough to paper one complete wall of my study. You learn certain lessons from this, apart from the obvious: if the plays aren't going to be produced, the material, at least, might be recycled. And, indeed, my first poems were speeches lifted from dud plays and delivered at poetry readings.

It must have been about 1971, when I'd started publishing poems and stories in magazines, that I was forced to confront what I was about as a writer. The confidence – and humiliation – of publication helps to concentrate the mind, as, indeed, did the business of performing the work in public. Avatar was a poetry-reading venue in Kensington, behind Gloucester Road, which I gravitated to once a month. It was presided over by an ancient titled Lady, and you were likely to run into famous poets, Sir John Waller being the most unlikely. Its abiding interest for me was that Avatar was my first meeting with the young American writer, Diana Hallett. Diana and I were soon to set up house in Shepherd's Bush and our fortunes were inextricable for the next decade.

What perhaps helped to motivate me, apart from the fact that I now lived in John Elsom's house, was my experience, fresh from a year in the Eastern Caribbean, directing the Caribbean Theatre Workshop. The four plays from that period are among those still to be revised. I had misjudged my audience in the Caribbean: in St Vincent I came over as someone privileged, from England. It was only the luck of sleeping in a haunted hotel in downtown Kingstown and not going mad when the jumbie appeared that gained me the necessary credibility. In

Trinidad I was held to be someone from England, but too radical to be let loose on a Port of Spain public in the wake of the recent attempted political coup. In Guyana, Georgetown theatre seemed to be in the very good hands of Ken Crosby and company. So I was seduced into becoming a volunteer on the grand project of building a highway through the interior of the country. The resulting play, *Down Mahda Way*, had two rehearsals in London but no public performance.

Prior to going to the Caribbean in 1970, I made belated contact with John La Rose from Trinidad who, with his wife Sarah White, had opened the New Beacon Bookshop in Finsbury Park, bringing Caribbean books, including non-Anglophone material and work relating to Latin America and Africa, to our attention. As the bookshop was in the front room of their home, the visitor was usually encouraged – with stimulating talk and the offer of a cup of tea/coffee and, sometimes, food – to hang about.

Caribbean literature wasn't exactly unknown to me in 1970. Over the preceding decade I'd read at random John Hearne and V. S. Naipaul as well as Jean Rhys' *Wide Sargasso Sea*. I'd struggled through much of Mittelholzer's Kaywana books and was entranced by Wilson Harris' *Palace of the Peacock*. In the late sixties Harris was a neighbour in Holland Park, and though we weren't acquainted, it was good for me to know that a substantial and visionary Caribbean presence was only a couple of hundred yards away.

My literary and academic background was something, I often felt, I was expected to apologise for. An A-level in economics was my only saving grace (other GCEs being Latin, Italian, English, History, Ancient History, etc.). Even my interests in kitchen sink drama or the Theatre of the Absurd were deemed to be 'English' tastes. People sometimes remonstrated with you, a man from the Third World, for not being a doctor or a lawyer or an engineer. Hence the value of my orientation course at John La Rose's bookshop.

Once, when asked why he wrote, John La Rose said: 'Because they lie about you. They pretend to speak for you and they lie about you.' I was encouraged by this, for I thought if anyone should lie about me, I should be accorded that privilege. Though I would aim, naturally, to tell the truth.

The crash course: Earl Lovelace, Alwyn Bennett, Austin Clarke and Derek Walcott – first encountered in *London Magazine* – came close to balancing all that Anglo-Saxon and Middle English. The excitement of recognising something of the texture of Caribbean living in the literature nevertheless occasioned a question mark in my mind. Much of the prose left me with a sense of sameness of experience which, though authentic, didn't quite capture the tone of my particular house in Montserrat. I read Lamming's *In the Castle of My Skin* and I agreed you couldn't write better than that. But was this my experience of growing up in the West Indies? It wasn't.

First of all I grew up with books in the house, lots of books that I was expected to work my way through. Alone, at night, in the drawing room at Harris, while my grandmother had her bath next door, I picked my way through John Bunyan and *Gulliver's Travels* and something called *John Halifax, Gentleman* – in the years before I was eleven. Gibbon's *Decline and Fall of the Roman Empire* was in the bookcase, though I didn't get round to that. And there was assorted religious material – not surprising with so many clergymen in the family. There was also a book in our bookcase called *Sinn Fein* – 'We Ourselves', as my brother translated. Montserrat was colonised in the 1620s by the Irish who proceeded to give the island that Columbus named in 1493 an Irish aspect which persisted even after the British claimed it.

My grandmother was head of the household. This wasn't unusual in the West Indies: when Andrew Salkey, in a poem, talks about the 'sea split marriage' he is talking about all of us. But even when the man of the house was around, she was head of the household and determined all our fortunes. She had a mythical status in the village; she was known as Queen Victoria and her house was popularly dubbed 'Government house'. I remember once when the Governor wrote to her, on some matter

of land registration, and signed off 'Your Humble Servant'. We
children had no doubt that this man, plump and plumed and
light-skinned, could be induced to bring my grandmother her
water in a ewer and to fill up her nightly bath tub. A bad leg
confined her to her room, but she still managed to control the
house and beyond that the estates. Hers was the family into
which my father had married. If he proved fallible, it was her
constancy that prevented us going to the dogs.

When I got back to England in 1971, among the rejected
manuscripts was one from the Royal Shakespeare Company
quibbling at the portrayal of the Black characters in a play I'd
submitted to them the previous year. The RSC seemed to have
no problem with the White characters, or with the theatrical
values of the piece. After the inevitable posture of being
affronted, I took a hard look at what I was doing. The father-
figure was not entirely convincing. I had known that at the time
of writing, and yet a sense of loyalty made me falsify his portrait.
I had introduced the father as a benign ghost, sitting in the
rocking chair in the drawing room, rocking the young son – me
– who was sitting on his knee. There was a story in the family
that after my father left (to go off to win World War Two) I
claimed the rocking chair and used to tip myself all the way
forward, without falling. The family apparently looked on, confident that an invisible hand – if not the father, the grandfather
behind him – kept me secure. That was the ghost figure I was
trying to portray. When I was directing the Caribbean Theatre
Workshop and struggling to create a convincing portrait of The
Father, I wrote a little poem which seemed to sum up my
difficulty at the time:

Another Dad

You're a fat old man
pleading for sympathy;

you huddle in the doorway
playing your instrument

badly – to embarrass me.
I'm your son, old man,

I'm your son
and will continue to look

the other way
till you learn to play better.

It was always difficult for me to imagine a male adult in the family, since I never had the experience of growing up in that environment. In our family the father was someone who neglected his family. But could you really call it neglect when the man went off to fight for Britain's freedom and was now a distinguished clergyman in Toronto? My brother much later supplied some of the details which would have fleshed out the portrait. Apparently when The Father returned from abroad to take over the family business after the death of my grandfather, he showed himself true to type. The business was running assorted scattered bits of land on which cotton was grown. But the man's interest was elsewhere. He had the flower-bed at the front of the house dug up in order to put in a new water cistern. That was the official story. In fact he was digging for buried treasure. Not finding it he had the hole filled in and the flower-bed replanted. The filled-in, replanted flower-bed settled down to being at least a foot lower than the rest of the yard, making it problematic for our cricket matches. The Father was a man who disturbed the order of the house, indeed, the aesthetic order of the house, and one was reluctant to explore fully the implications of this. Meanwhile, The Father's original continued to hide behind his clerical collar, a Very Reverend in Toronto.

Whose family is it anyway? Is it the writer's to write about or the members' to live? I accept, of course, that a writer of power and conviction must create a fictional world that is large enough to live in. I feel that the space inherited from this family is so vast that it seems physical. When I was growing up with my grandmother, in Harris, such bedtime stories as were told weren't about Anancy or Aesop, they were about the family, the progress that her eight brothers and sisters had made in the world, the doctor in Boston, the lawyer in New York, the Justice of the Peace who went twice to England and had some sharp things to say about the state of order on the streets of London. So the role of family chronicler was one that someone had to take on. Though family members were suspicious of my willingness to do it.

My brother Norman sends me newspaper cuttings and rings me with information about the house in Montserrat which he thinks I might have forgotten. And he's right. Being the youngest of four children I became fully aware of the house after it had passed its peak, so to speak. Mine is an emptyish house occupied by my grandmother and myself, along with Sarah, a young girl who worked for us and slept in. Occasionally a neighbour, a young man from the village, would sleep in the spare room when we were nervous of burglars. That was during the week. At weekends the rest of the family would come back from Plymouth – where my brothers and sister were at school – and, of course, during the holidays. Then I would be relegated to relative insignificance.

But this is 1997; I am in Sheffield. My brother rang me a few nights ago from London: did I remember the bookshelf at the bottom of the stairs, in the corner of the dining room, leading up to the drawing room? Initially, no, but on reflection, yes. The steps leading up to the drawing room brought something else to life. It was from those steps that I first heard my brother declaim Mark Antony's great speech, his tribute to the newly murdered Caesar, I in the dining room representing the 'market-place', reacting like a Roman to the oration from the pulpit. He's halfway up the stairs, half turned (so he's going up) looking down on us. But that's long ago. What role is he playing now, Norman, forty years on, ringing me up from London? Not Mark Antony. Did I remember, in the corner at the foot of the stairs, inset in the wall, a ledge, a cool spot where each day Sarah placed a jar of fresh water, covered with a saucer or maybe with a white linen cloth? There were books on the shelf above the alcove. In his time, in my brother's time, someone used to read to my grandmother after her bath, at night, and one of the books they read was *Paradise Lost*, taken from that shelf.

This news was intriguing because although the reading to my grandmother continued in my time, we certainly never read *Paradise Lost*. I wasn't even aware of it in the house. We read from the newspaper, careful to mispronounce words like 'rape' that we were not supposed to know; we read passages from John Bunyan and things like that, but mostly, of course, from the Bible. Every new revelation about those times makes me think I've fallen down on the job. It also reinforces the feeling that I'd missed out on the best of the house, that the main actors had done their thing before us and that my sister and I were merely understudies.

Equally intriguing are the missives from my brother, the newspaper cuttings that arrive every three weeks or so. This is general, 'improving' information, addressed to the professor (my status of academic still outweighs my profession of writer). Among recent offerings: someone claiming to be able to teach Americans to speak a foreign language overnight; an article challenging the fundamentalists on creation; the crisis in Korea; David Edgar on 'New Writing'. The relationship between Antony and the Crowd has shifted over the years. My brother is both audience and mentor. As audience he used occasionally to come to my poetry readings in the seventies and eighties. He buys my books to give as presents. When he sees them in the shops he rings me up and talks sales. Part of his input is to hint at new things I might write.

And now I have an ungenerous thought: my brother must recognise himself in some of my fiction, for comic characteristics are taken from people I know, including family. Could it be that with these cuttings he is working to modify the image of the family I present?

Wilson Harris apart, whom I didn't really know, the few West Indian writers I'd come across in Britain seemed not to have had my experience of growing up in the region, or to be dismissive of it. So I convinced myself that they, too, were lying about me. It wasn't just my own little experience being invisibilised that made me uneasy. What of all the other families like us? West Indians and West Indianness were being defined in terms of lack or absence, or being on the periphery. That was OK, that was fine; true in a sense, though all these things *together* might not be accurate. The problem was what this was being defined against. Against England. Britain. Against an idea of English-ness, preserved by us – preserved along with, as I discovered later, the good people of New Zealand.

My experience of England wasn't that of plenty, despite Mr Macmillan's 'You've never had it so good' election slogan. The living standard of our family had declined in England: we didn't run a car, my mother no longer had a chauffeur, we didn't live in a house of twelve rooms with four others to our name, we didn't have servants. There was no pining for any of this – except by my mother, and she didn't go on about it – but it was an unspoken fact between us.

And in our early contacts here people didn't correspond to our notion of 'The English'. The family who rented our down-stairs front room were rag-and-bone people (with children our age who eventually had to be ejected because we feared for our own hygiene). They were in line, we believe, for one of the last ten-pound-assisted passages to Australia. They were replaced by a businessman who conducted his business on the pavement. He took bets on the horses, for until Macmillan legal-ised the activity in time to help him win the 1959 General Election, punters had to do their trade on the pavements. But this was a definite step up because wife and daughter were respectably turned out and the daughter was also a student.

In between we had an odd experience which made us reluc-tant to think all things ill of the West Indies. One Christmas Eve my brother Norman set off to the West End – maybe to Covent Garden – where you could get the turkey at half-price or less. On his travels in the West End for the turkey he ran into a woman and child in distress. They were homeless. The husband had been violent, and they had been housed in separate places of refuge. The mother and child had left their refuge and were on the street. It was cold. It was Christmas. Norman knew that my mother would welcome someone like that in the house at Christmas. So he extended the invitation on my mother's behalf.

My mother thought that was entirely proper, but what to do if the violent husband turned up? For Norman admitted that the wife was seeking to contact the husband. We were still debating this when the knocker went and the woman turned up, with her child. We took them in, fed them, and I, being the youngest, had to give up my bed to the mother and child and share a bed with my brother. The husband later turned up – very pleasant and contrite and hungry – and thanked us for looking after his family (my memory is faulty: it is they rather than the rag-and-bone people who were destined for Australia) before going back to his refuge. But the next morning, the mother, with her child, disappeared, having stolen my mother's purse.

I remember debates in the house in Ladbroke Grove from 1956 and leading up to the 1959 General Election. We were politically unsophisticated in an English setting, having been rightish rather than leftish in a West Indian context, our large-mindedness, I realised later, being nearer to paternalism than I'd like to admit. My mother liked Mr Eden's command of English. Someone on the radio complained that Mr Macmillan, who succeeded him, was guilty of splitting his infinitives, and this was noted with interest in our house. Leaving that aside Mr Macmillan's bad teeth (clearly discernible on television) didn't appeal. These were the debates we assumed to be taking place in homes all over Britain.

We were a little bit cut off because we were in our own house. My mother had insisted on that. Not for her to be at the mercy of other people, the stony faced landladies and landlords photographed behind signs saying NO COLOUREDS, NO IRISH, NO DOGS. (We were grateful that the Irish were included, but embarrassed about the dogs.) My mother had sent on the money to my elder brothers who were barely in their twenties to buy a house. We didn't know any other West Indian families in this situation and that meant stray students and other friends from home found their way to our place, mainly at weekends, to re-experience something of the warmth of home. So it was here in late-fifties England that our re-education took place, and in 1959 some members of our family registered their first Labour vote. We quite liked Gaitskell, though we preferred Nye Bevan, because his odd-sounding Welsh voice assured us that you could be fluent in English without aping the vowels which made us sound odd. Much later, of course, Linton Kwesi Johnson, the dub poet, came to the same conclusion via John Arlott, the celebrated cricket commentator whose Somerset burr emphasised that there was more than one acceptable form of spoken English.

We couldn't avoid the more overt politics of the time; there was a sense, almost, of being targeted, with Oswald Mosley coming to the door. In Montserrat, in Plymouth, my mother used to sit at the upstairs window in our house in Parliament Street, looking down on the world. In our house in Ladbroke Grove she assumed the same posture. It was from here, in 1959, that she effectively attended an Oswald Mosley rally. His message was the familiar one: we West Indians were children who had been misled into coming to England. The streets of England were not paved with gold. We were unhappy to be here. It was unfair to ask us to remain in a place where we were cold and unhappy. The best thing was to send us back to a place that was warm and where we could be happy once again. That was his political programme.

We were struck by his politeness: was it right, was it a misuse of language to call it politeness? Would we rather have such ideas delivered in a reasonable tone or with the thuggishness they concealed? The crowd seemed reasonably relaxed, both assent and indignation muted. Someone in the crowd whispered that Mosley looked Jewish. Next door to us lived Geoffrey Hamm, Mosley's right-hand man in the area.

My mother, unflinching, looked down on Mosley from her window; a cousin newly in the army stood at the back of the crowd in his uniform, his arms folded. A few other West Indians stood impassive, refusing to be provoked. I joined my mother at the window. I had a sense then of a space to protect and thought, with the posture of my mother, with my army cousin in the crowd, with the calmness of the 'boys' whom we didn't know, that we wouldn't be panicked into anything, certainly not into flight. I'm talking about a view of England. It seemed shortsighted to use England as the only, or main, frame of reference when trying to bring the West Indies into focus. So I vary the frame of reference. England hasn't been my only home from home.

But why exactly do I write? It's not just self-aggrandisement. It's not even, with respect to conversations at the New Beacon Bookshop, because I want to answer back. No, it's more personal, less reactive. Back in the 1950s when I was putting press studs in belts a choice of career seemed open. One boss at the time, G. G. Spencer, liked my work and suggested – who knows how seriously? – a partnership in the belt firm in Great Portland Street. And briefly, I did see myself as head of a leather and suede empire, belting women – average waist twenty-two inches – from Canada to Nigeria. And yet I didn't want to be consigned to the rag trade. So Spencer and I talked futures, careers. For no particular reason I said to him one day that I wanted to be a doctor. But medicine was the wrong profession for me he said because I didn't have the necessary love of people.

We didn't discuss this much over belts, but I couldn't entirely dislodge the feeling that I harboured a political rather than an instinctive feel for people. This contributed to my going to university to read Philosophy and eventually to saying rude things about Plato and Walter Pater. (Was it squeamishness rather than pain that moved me to other people's suffering? Could I get away with defining squeamishness as an aesthetic quality?) When, later, towards the end of the Nigerian Civil War, Nnamdi Azikwe, the renowned ex-president of the republic, switched from supporting the losing Biafran side, he gave a curious reason: he deplored, finally, the aesthetic spectacle of filling the world's television screens with Africans humiliating Africans, Black women humiliated, Black children brutalised, dying of kwashaqua. He appealed for an end to the war on aesthetic grounds. I felt both vindicated and appalled. I have tried ever since, through writing, to penetrate my own layers of protective skin. I write, quite simply – and it's not simple – to make myself more human.

Attia Hosain

❖❖❖❖❖❖❖❖❖❖❖❖❖❖❖

Deep Roots

Sadly, Attia Hosain died while this book was in the process of being put together. The piece that follows is an amalgam of her last piece of original writing (specifically for this collection) and a 1956 broadcast that had been read aloud during her last public appearance some months before.

Deep Roots shows the meticulous quality of her very finely-tuned mind. Attia Hosain's fiction, long out of print and recently reprinted by Virago, is the product of a determined pioneer. Born into aristocracy in Lucknow, she became the first woman of her class to graduate. Inspired by left-wing politics, she wrote for journals in India before coming to Britain in the 1940s. The trigger for her turn to fiction, and the compromises that writing in English posed for her, are described in her piece.

As a child, I remember a tree growing in my home, very deeply rooted, with strong wide branches that seemed to cover a whole world. Its leaves and bark were used for healing, and it provided a wonderful cool shade, as the wind passed through its branches, making the leaves dance in the breeze. I think that is how I identify myself, with my life spanning two civilisations and cultures and many, many histories.

My mother came from a family of scholars, not from the feudal *taluqdars* of my father's family. One side of our home was my mother's domain, wholly part of an Indian culture, where we studied Persian and Arabic and Urdu poetry. Through

a door and a hall was the Western side, my father's. He had
studied at Cambridge and the Inns of Court in the previous
century. His English friends came to our home in Lucknow, not
the condescending 'imperialist' breed, but people who loved
India, its heritage, art and culture. There was no division
between the two elements in my home; rather a flow of life,
acceptance and interdependence. We lived in many centuries, it
seemed, moving across them in moments.

But though English was so familiar, it was at the same time
not my mother tongue, Urdu. Then why should I write in it? I
spoke English from the age of three when I was put in the
charge of an English governess, and then, when I was five, went
to a school primarily for English and Anglo-Indian girls. At that
time in India the best modern education was only possible in
such schools. From then on until I graduated fourteen years
later, I was taught the same subjects as in any English school. I
learnt the beauty, rhythm, flexibility and richness of the English
language from reading the Bible, Chaucer, Milton and Shakespeare. I spoke my own language and lived with it at home,
but I was taught it only in the time that could be spared from
studying for the examinations. This is how I formed the habit
of reading, writing and even thinking in English. In fact, I think
in both languages – but there were more occasions to think in
English. My vocabulary in my mother tongue was limited –
and more so because the pressure of other studies constantly
interrupted my studies of our own classics, of Arabic and
Persian.

Many Indians grew up like me, at the best bilingual and at
the worst almost ignorant of their mother tongue. The climate
of opinion and the system of education that created this situation
was the result of all sorts of complicated forces – political, economic and social. At that time, too, the relation between rulers
and ruled in India was changing rapidly and at the moment
that the two cultures began to clash openly, Western influences
were beginning to penetrate established ways of living and
thinking. There was, no doubt, some snobbery involved – at

least in some cases – in the imitation and adoption of English ways and speech: but there was also a progressive element in it because in the struggle for freedom English was both a weapon as well as the key to what I might call the ideological arsenal.

As far as I myself was concerned, although I was educated in English and my family adopted certain English ways, I was brought up very conscious of our own culture, our feudal background and relationships. I grew up with the English language but not with the culture behind it. I was always outside that and deeply rooted in my own.

I have described my background because it explains the paradoxical difficulty of writing in a foreign language. Obviously, these difficulties aren't ones of grammar and syntax – I learned those rules young enough to forget them. No, the difficulty lies here – that unless one is completely part of a culture there are always limitations to one's use of a language because it is not bred in one's bones and so one misses certain subtleties; colloquialisms and dialects remain unfamiliar. And all this means that one cannot be completely at ease, can't play about with words without self-consciousness coming as a shadow between one and the reader.

In fact, when you write in a foreign language, you begin to realise how much it is given life by the culture behind it. It is born, grows, changes – and dies – with the people who use it to communicate their thoughts and desires. Its words are created as symbols of those very thoughts and desires. And writing in a foreign language, you come to realise how words create not only a single image but a series of images so that if the image created in the mind of the writer is different from the image in the mind of the reader, there will not be complete understanding between them.

My first writing took the form of journalism. I had been very influenced by the political thoughts of the Left in the Progressive Writers' Movement, through my friends Mulk Raj Anand, Sajjad Zaheer and Shabzada Mahmuduzaffar, and was asked by

Desmond Young to write for *The Pioneer*, the historic newspaper he edited.

But it was in Britain that I turned to fiction. My husband was posted to the Indian High Commission in London in 1947, before India became independent. I was so excited to be travelling at last to those parts of the world where I had travelled so long in my thoughts and imagination. I had lived in them through the words of its great writers and philosophers, seen them through the eyes of artists and heard them through its musicians. In London, I walked along roads that seemed completely known and familiar, read the names on plaques of writers and artists who had made these surroundings resonant in my mind.

Reality, in its physical shape, was very different. This was also London in the aftermath of war, where streets were dark early, where there were gaps in bomb-damaged buildings and strict rationing. Yet I enjoyed each simple encounter. There was, then, a bond that grew out of shared hardships; no hostility, rather an eagerness to talk to someone from part of the world where many had been sent, as a kind of extension of experience. I too had had family and friends fighting that war, in Africa, in Burma, the Middle East and Europe. Not many still remember that India had the largest volunteer army in two world wars.

In 1947, earlier than expected, came Independence and the Partition of the subcontinent of India. Together with the raising of flags and celebrations came the enforced migrations of more millions than ever before, of massacres and infinite loss. That we were in London did not lessen the anguish. It sharpened it. There was no family from which to draw strength, no advice beyond rumour and a cold definition of statistics.

My mind could not accept the division of India, nor could I have belief in the logistics and legalities which subsumed the ideals of freedom and Independence. What then became of choices? There were not just two – India and Pakistan – but a third, Britain. There was to be no renouncing of nationality; everyone from the Indian subcontinent had British passports in 1947. We had a legal right to be British citizens, which I exercised. I respected the country which had given me not just physical refuge but had an ideology of human rights and civil liberties to which I was completely attuned. At the same time, I respected and obeyed the laws of the country of my birth where I was recognised to have the rights of someone of Indian origin.

Above all, Britain was the neutral area where I could still meet those from whom we were now divided by borders of nationality and an artificially nurtured hostility. Family separated from family, friend from friend.

Perhaps, sub-consciously, to console myself for the maiming sense of loss of identity, I began to write. In this at least, I had the best of both my worlds.

A kind friend, whose family and friends had been refugees from the Nazis, liked my stories and took them to an agent, Joyce Wiener. She became a friend and encouraged me to write. So, in this new country, I found myself in contact with the world of words and writing that had formed me from my earliest years. Leonard Woolf had wanted to publish the stories first in the Hogarth Press, which filled me with humility and joy. When I went to meet Cecil Day Lewis, whose poetry I used to read in the thirties, at Chatto and Windus, he told me that Chatto was publishing my novel not because I was a storyteller from a new land but because they thought I deserved to be published, and I felt an even greater happiness. He also taught me a lesson about the value of brevity, and of putting thoughts into focus. He had questioned the length of some of my chapters that mainly concerned political developments. 'That is the way life was!' I remember protesting. Life, he pointed out however, was different from Art. I cut my manuscript drastically.

The stories that I kept on writing in my head were always to do with the problems of human relationships, dilemmas in the context of social and political and philosophical conditions – problems I knew best, like my own breath, from my family's eight hundred years in India. The book I began but did not finish was a bridge between that background, through the partition of the country, and to the strands of Indian lives in England.

It was while writing that I became more conscious of deep cultural differences existing, even when there was no difficulty in forming relationships of any kind with people of another country. They manifested themselves particularly in language.

What is one to do if a concept or an image of one's own culture is so alien to the foreign culture that no word for it exists in that language? That is the gravest problem of all. My own difficulties arose out of this, both in the handling of words and in the search for related images.

Of course these difficulties are directly related to the subject of one's work, to its form and content. English is still used on the subcontinent as a means of communication because there is a wide field of common thought. But a great silent gap remains. There comes a point beyond which the two cultures can neither clash nor merge nor come to terms with each other. And in writing my first novel, I became painfully aware of the inadequacy of the words I was using when I came up against that silent gap. And there is no avoiding it if one wishes to write with sincerity and truth. For difficulties of expression arise not in dealing with emotions or experiences that are universal, they arise when they are related to the cultural pattern.

So what does one do? If the language lacks the words to express the images of another then one either has to find related images or explain them. To say the least, this is a curb on the creative process, and artistically destructive. An unnatural element is introduced between the writer and the free flow of creative thought. One stops being a creative writer and becomes a translator, and in the process of translation one becomes conscious of the reader at the cost of the characters one is creating. They begin to lose life and become puppets.

Writing dialogue presents its own special problems. I find myself thinking in dialogue in my own language and translating my thoughts literally. That sets off a chain reaction of difficulties. First of all, phrases that sound natural in my mother tongue sound artificial or ornate in translation. This is partly because the language of a very ancient culture such as ours is compounded of many cultures and allusions to myths, legends; philosophical and religious beliefs become part of one's everyday speech. But most of these are strange to the West. Again, in the society about which I have written, it is natural for cultured people to quote couplets from Persian, Urdu or Hindi to make a point. Their choice of these quotations and the way in which they use them are an indication of character and establish their background in the same way as turns of phrase, the misuse of words or colloquialisms and dialects. But how can I explain these allusions or how can I translate these couplets without explanation? If I explain, the artistic expression is destroyed. In fact, there are many painful moments when I have to remind myself that I am writing neither a guidebook nor a sociological survey, nor a collection of strange and fantastic customs – that a novel is not a place for explanations of this kind.

Then, take the example of certain significant words. There are particular Urdu words which establish the relationship between two people. But to convey this in English there is only the pronoun 'you', since 'thou' has become archaic. Somehow I have to use this for three pronouns, each with its special significance. In Urdu, 'aap' is used to address one's elders and betters in a formal sense and sometimes sarcastically. 'Tum' is used for those younger, equals and inferiors. 'Tu' is used to address inferiors, loved ones, and God. That it is used both to express contempt and also the highest form of love is an indication of the subtle shades acquired by a word in an old language. 'Tu' has connotations that make it relate to mystic philosophy – the same philosophy which has made wine, unholy in itself in Islam, the symbol of the love of God.

This complicated pattern of relationships in a feudal society between individuals, between them and society, between men and women, seems almost impossible to transfer into English speech.

Then there is the relationships of the sexes. In the West, 'purdah' or the seclusion of women, is taken to be the outward sign of that relationship. But 'purdah' is not merely a physical fact. What is important is the structure of thought and social habit behind it. When I write in English that a wife and husband do not address each other by name or do not appear to talk together nor to their children in the presence of elders, it appears curious, maybe ridiculous. But all this was part of a pattern of thought and behaviour – how deeply part of it can be understood when we consider that in classical poetry it was the convention that the beloved should always be addressed in the masculine gender by poets. It was indelicate to do otherwise.

The very different attitude to marriage from the Western one follows as a natural consequence from the attitude to love and the relationship of the sexes. For example, if I wish to describe the emotional reactions of the bride when she is leaving her home at a certain point after the Muslim marriage ceremony, two key Urdu words alone are enough to evoke the images I want to project. One is 'susral'. By definition 'susral' is the home into which a woman is married, but it connotes a whole pattern of duties, responsibilities and renunciations, and a code of behaviour in relation to the family into which one is married, including its servants and dependants.

The other word is 'babul' – the song sung at the moment of the bride's departure for her 'susral'. Literally, it is merely a bride's song of farewell, full of pathos and tenderness and deeply moving. But a whole way of life leads up to that moment of departure – and the song is a symbol of it. The parting symbolises more than the feelings that enter in when a Western bride leaves her home. You may understand the implications of parting, in that particular pattern of life, if I tell you that the word 'jahez' which means 'dowry' is also closely related to the word 'tajheiz', used in connection with the last rites for the dead. How can one explain that, as part of the whole complex, there is no cruelty in the concept?

At the same time, I could never have written so truthfully

about Britain and the British as I did about India. I see that as a limitation. Perhaps it was because I was always an observer, watching through glass, never really made to feel at home as in the Eastern tradition. I could have described what I saw, but I could not penetrate that invisible barrier to enter into a 'self' other than the polite exterior.

I feel that I belong to another age, an age becoming part of history. The second and third generations, perhaps because of the seamless nature of the crossover, have created their own transliterations of influences. The vitality of writers like Salman Rushdie, Anita Desai, Vikram Seth, Amitabha Ghosh and Alan Sealy is markedly due to the fusion of so many voices and influences.

However one lives, one can live simply as a human being, among other human beings. Here I am, I have chosen to live in this country which has given me so much. But I cannot get out of my blood the fact I had the blood of my ancestors for eight hundred years in another country, and I am still that person.

I am sad that I did not complete the books I have begun, or hoped to write, about the terrible pain when a country and a people are divided. It is never just a physical division, but a cutting apart of human beings.

It is only with the written word that one can reach out to people to let them know they are not alone. But that sense of aloneness is often heightened when people who have never 'crossed frontiers', or never needed to do so, deny one a sense of belonging anywhere. They are not aware of the sense of solitude one can experience when, alone in space, reaching out for those 'speaking one's own language' of tolerance and under- standing, one seeks to balance consciousness of one's roots with a sense of belonging to the whole world.

B. A. Gilroy

◆◆◆◆◆◆◆◆◆◆◆◆◆◆◆◆◆

Waltzing Across Four and a Half Decades

Beryl Gilroy was among the many British Guyanese who came to Britain to study. She combined a long and successful teaching career with her novel-writing. Now retired, her memoirs *Black Teacher* is a classic of its kind. Her historical novels set in the Caribbean evoke both a powerful sense of place and time with great delicacy and accuracy, and explore romantic relations between the races. As an educationalist she made invaluable contributions to the debate on language and the Caribbean child in British schools.

I arrived as a student in Britain five years after World War Two ended. Britain was in a process of reconstruction. Black people, then popularly called 'Niggers' or 'Spades', consisted of pre-war Black families, leftover Indian sailors called Lascars, Ayahs or old Indian women (sometimes seen in the East End markets) brought over as servants from India and then abandoned, colonial sailors and war veterans who had formed liaisons with White women during or soon after the war.

Student life was a life apart. Universities were élitist and students valued education – especially British education, which we were proud to pursue. Under the aegis of the Crown Agents who arranged grants, fees, and other money matters, the Colonial Office, whose officials liaised with universities, and the

British Council who arranged the social side of our lives, we took our work very seriously indeed.

Our passages, in or out of England, were booked through the Crown Agents, and the worst disgrace of all was to fail exams. I was one of two thousand students bound for British universities – two of us in London. We didn't know what to expect. A college of London University existed in Jamaica. A few of us had read of universities. The word excited us, gave heat to the icy rain – made us surprised at the sight of 'white men working' and talking English incomprehensible to us.

I lived in a village prior to training as a teacher. We were the first home-grown teachers. Our village adjoined a sugar plantation at the end of the Corentyne Coast, a densely populated area with a string of villages and plantations dotted along the extent of the coastline. When, aged 12, I attended the Anglican school, I was in a class of about sixty children aged between 12 and 14. We represented all the six races in our village. A polychromatic mix, we all sang 'When Morning Fills the Skies' at our morning assembly, and 'The Day Thou Gavest, Lord, is Ended' each afternoon at the close of school.

Nobody protested. We kept our school culture and our home cultures apart, but everybody celebrated Christmas, Ramadan, the Diwali festival of the Hindus and the Chinese New Year. At Christmas we all went to the Goat Race, the Boat Race and watched the Masqueraders and Jon Kanu dancers and their attendants, Long-lady who danced on stilts, as well as Waxy Nanny, whose gaudy skirt hid an enormous bamboo frame.

Ritual had not died out in Black families. We were educated about Black history by the elders of the Negro Progress Convention. We were taught songs of slavery – told its stories and learned the apt proverbs that came out of the imposition of African, Spanish, French and other words upon English. There was a Black culture until 1938.

All the children in our village played cricket on the sands, but girls disappeared from the games as we got older. Life was understandable. Children's work helped the family economy, and education was the road that took us to opportunity. Black oral history died with the old folk.

Politics in our village centred around simple choices like whether British Guyana should be a 'crown colony or not', whether the work of the Legislative Council was being fair enough, and the poison of oppression on the sugar plantations and price fixing for rice and coconuts by the Government. I did not know of, and had never heard of, the racial politics for which British Guyana – now Guyana – is today famous. On a visit a few years ago, I was staggered by the racism in the Caribbean. Those who were giving it willy-nilly would be the first to howl about it in Britain. Racism – the scourge of our time! It isn't only what Whites do to Blacks. The Caribbean colour-shade racism flourishes! I did not know the term. It was what they called prejudice in those days and I understood it to mean a kind of rejection Whites showed to Blacks at every opportunity, when Blacks were subject to plantation rules and life.

In Britain in the fifties Black faces were few, but as time went on, they became more visible. The children stopped one to ask the time, in order to be sure one spoke English, and did not make monkey sounds. Sometimes they asked, 'Please see me across the road'. And when the reply was, 'Of course, come along', their faces lit up.

In my studies, school visits, school practice, and my work in child guidance, 'childhood' was still alive. Children had regular television-free lives, and came to school rested and ready to work for the Eleven Plus.

I had been used to 'whole class teaching' of large numbers of children using rudimentary facilities. The schoolrooms, even after the war, were places of abundance compared to those in my country. We used 'from home' books, called Royal Readers, and they contained concepts which could never be formed by children who had never seen Autumn, Winter, a hearth, etc. Imagine my surprise when I could, at last, associate those words with their true reality.

During my studies a woman who'd worked overseas introduced me to evening classes. I bought *Floodlight* for six shillings – a small compact book in which I found that three terms of study cost between thirty shillings and two pounds. Grants were small and money borrowed from our Government had to be paid back. Many of us worked during the holidays or baby-sat for the families – mostly Jewish – who gave friendship and support to lonely students.

My landlady encouraged me to study in evening classes if I wanted to fill the gaps in my own education. I began my paper-chase. It drove away homesickness. I was excited by opportunity, and overwhelmed by possibilities. I was the hungry rat in an oversupplied granary. But my own course was coming to an end and I wanted to make a real bid for a job as a UN field-worker. To meet all my criteria I needed to get a job.

I by-passed the Colonial Office and applied for a teaching job. I was dead lucky. I ran into the ex-principal of the Training College in Georgetown. He thought me a gifted teacher and had placed many opportunities my way. He recommended me to the D.E.S. (the Department of Education and Science) and I was told to wait until my country was contacted.

It was a stressful time. Mercifully I was still considered a student and went, as I had always done, to socialise with other West Indian students who lived at the British Council Hostel in Hans Crescent, London. The British landlady was at that time reluctant to accommodate Black men.

Hans Crescent was a real social centre and the venue for weekend dances, Christmas balls, lectures and discussions. All the great politicians of the time came to lecture and enlighten us as to the possible benefits that Independence would bring. They all talked Independence. Nkrumah of the Gold Coast, Owolowo and Chief Azikwe of Nigeria, C.L.R. James, Peter Blackman, Eric Williams, Norman Manley, Forbes Burnham and many more talked persuasively about Freedom from the British. Today hundreds wish the British would return, although Independence was a time of rejoicing. Can not someone explain to those who wantonly maim and destroy that consequences follow?

At first nobody admitted that the colonies had become too expensive for post-war Britain and Macmillan's 'Wind Of Change' speech was saying just that. But the colonies wanted 'Independence'. They thought Britain would 'go' but continue to pay. The race was on for the Gold Coast to be next after India and Sri Lanka. I was not sure whether my work, concerned with Child Guidance, Play Therapy and Developmental Psychology, would find a place in British Guyana, where children were taught a strict syllabus and promoted only when they passed from one 'standard' to another. Politics opposed my thinking about helping those who need help regardless of race. Children in Britain at that era of the Eleven Plus were silently selected 'as possible Eleven Plus material' at about six years of age by various Head Teachers in schools I visited. There were few – very few indeed – Black school children in British schools, but the assumption was that middle-class children were more likely than working-class children to pass the Eleven Plus. I continued my paperchase. In the winter months studying and work became harder.

Teaching in Britain

While I waited for my appointment and allocation to a school, I worked all over the place, to enlarge my experience of another culture, gather insight and flesh out my encounters with decent, enlightened English people. A confident and self-assured people, aware of their traditions and familiar with the words of the National Anthem and *Jerusalem*, taught to us at school. My headmaster was an Anglophile and taught us traditional British songs: We even sang the Eton Boat Song, although none of us knew who or what Eton was.

After months I was called to interview. Men and women prodded me about my reasons for wanting to study and work here. I was as articulate then as I am now, and when asked about the basic subjects, I was on home ground. One of my interviewers was a Miss Blackmore who had been the principal of the Carnegie Centre. We learned home-making, a kind of mimesis of the British kitchen culture. I cannot remember our home-grown products being considered. One day – unexpectedly – I was called to the London County Council Divisional Office and after many false starts sent to a Church school. I liked to work in Roman Catholic schools: one nun, Sister Consulata, always asked for me during my teacher training. She was a wonderful teacher and served as my role model.

I left my RC placement after a year when children of other religions – too young to cross a busy arterial road – were sent to us. I spent one day in the next school and five years in the third school. It was there that many good things happened to me, although when visitors came to visit this new post-war school, the head teacher *always* prepared them for my difference. I left the school for family life and remained children- and house-bound for ten years.

By 1965 I returned to part-time teaching. The school I was sent to was overrun with colonial children – many described as mentally deficient and put in special schools. The children, rushed into Britain, were disorientated when they came to me. They did not understand 'talk', nor were they able to locate themselves in space and time. Their first contact with White people was not always positive, productive or understandable.

Black children called for change in scripts and attitude, and many teachers did not want change. A few children passed the Eleven Plus, but their parents failed the interview. When asked, 'Would you be able to keep your children in school for seven years', they replied, 'If God lets me, and my family situation stays the same'. They should have said, 'Yes'. Some did not attend the interviews at all. It called for special clothes, special manners and talk and special action. They didn't want to shame their children, talk bruk-mouth (broken English) and be pinned by those blue eyes 'like sausage deh pon stick'.

Each day, beginning 3 October 1953, I wrote my journal and

this was how I highlighted the problems of 'reading'. It was heartbreaking to watch the mental and perceptive dislocation, the incomprehension and the struggle of Jamaican and Cypriot children to make sense of the books they read, and their frustration when they failed to turn words into concepts.

The children removed themselves from reality. The Greeks smiled, the Indians turned on stranger Muslims, the West Indians bounced up and down, were inattentive and got labelled as disruptive. They longed for outdoors. School confined them and made them negate their bodies. White parents and children were blatantly anti-foreign. Keep Britain White was the war cry. Although some Black male writers had published books, they said little of value to the rulers of empire. Jan Carew had published *Black Midas*, Braithwaite had written several books, *To Sir With Love* and *Choice of Straws*, John Heane, George Lamming and Naipaul had also been published, but the women, oh no! They were peripheral to White women, who were peripheral to White men. Only Sylvia Smith had managed it.

From my work in UNICEF Guyana, I knew that active reading, humorous poetry and art could link children with the past. Reading should be therapeutic and relevant. I designed 'News Time'. Children talked of what bothered them, what they saw on the way to school, about school itself, about me – a foreigner trying to teach them in a language they hardly knew. The children needed the past – the people they had left behind.

In order for reading to progress, we had to keep records and list the pages read each day. The books we used were *Janet and John*, written for White Australians, and easily transportable to White Britain after World War Two. Another series was called *Dick and Dora* – both dull and repetitive. I began to script little stories with the children's news as the centre. We discussed the stories and gave each child a list of his own words. Many of the words formed part of everyone's experience. For example:

There is a tree by John's house
It is an apple tree

John has an apple tree
By his house

We had extracted the 'key' words has, his, house, tree, etc. and put them on cards for reinforcement. The interest in reading grew. When individuals had done their 'set' reading, they could read our books. We knew that reading English did not necessarily mean understanding it.

As a result of these play-books, I was invited into the *Nippers* team. *Nippers* came out of the psycho-social lives of children. We observed the children, spoke to them and wrote the stories they gave us. *Nippers* sold millions worldwide and children adored them. My grand-daughter's school has a full set, and even so many years after their discontinuance, children read them and decide on their favourite ones. I believe that children must connect emotionally with text. In the *Nippers* series we treated race minimally. Integration was expected to take care of race. We were concerned with class. The working classes have the same struggle against the linguistic irrelevance of text as Black children. Reading calls for basic skills formed when children focus, concentrate and learn to like words and become aware of their nature and their power. People who only learn phonic reading methods must not only be systematically taught to spell but given help in comprehension.

Television is magical – things happen so quickly, the process is difficult to follow, interpret and learn. Children bring the same fleeting visual involvement to text. They fail to notice difference. I know this because I am involved with 'special needs'.

I have written several series of readers, now only obtainable in libraries. My novels were written over the years. I did not submit many to publishers because their readers were opinion 'addicts' and 'Anancy men' of the Caribbean who 'read' for publishers. I have always written books I want to write – books that celebrate historical Black women, that record our traditions, our humour and the way we are. Mimesis affects only some of us.

I have opposed racism for many years because of the psychological constructs I brought with me. My village gave me identity of place, family, religion and group. I had an educational identity. I was always able to express my identity in my work, as a teacher, in writing and in attitude. I feel no need to eulogise 'Empire'. It was all I knew and we were all making our way mainly by our own efforts.

Today, however, as I reach other milestones, I must cope with identities created for me by people who know nothing of me. Like Stephen Lawrence, and those who die in the holding cells – or rather contemporary slave pens – people see only our difference. Because they fear it, it brings out their intellectual bestiality and they permit themselves to construct stereotypes with which to suffocate the intellectual mobility of some foreigners too obviously honed in on success.

In years to come, the attitudes brought in by newcomers will surface and be unleashed on the old, the poor, and the different. I hope not because Britain is essentially a decent place to take refuge and find acceptance.

Conclusion

Finally I want to comment on the changes I have observed over my 45 years here.

The children of the first-wave immigrants – professionals seeking self-betterment – have done well. We kept together, discussed and sought the best for our children. A few were sent back home to be educated when the odds seemed too great.

Those children of manual workers, women alone, and those who were left to struggle for survival, must also be commended for hanging on and never losing sight of their goals.

The men always have a harder time. The gender mythologies of libido, morbido and cogito persist. They are performance men. They can dance at the drop of a hat, get stoned on drugs, but grasp chances to sex women. I do not understand how so many Black men stay sane, look after their children and strive to walk beside them.

As a member of the North Metropolitan Committee of the Race Relations Board, we dealt with blatant racisms, and helped to create opportunities. Today economic racism has become subterranean. Saying 'We are Equal Opportunities employers' means nothing. We must ask who gets the £4 an hour jobs? The scholarships at universities to which the Euro-tribe and South African Whites flock? We must seek out the bigots from wherever they are – even those above the law.

Racism must be provable and the only way this can be done would be through 'surveillance cameras' in places where Blacks are negated, sedimented and persecuted each day 'just for fun'.

Racism is the product of impenetrable or hermetically sealed minds. We can never escape those minds. They have the capacity to reproduce themselves endemically. They are unmindful of experience and bondaged by power-needs and ethnic falsehoods. Black is a fearsome colour to them.

Our children will, in the future, judge the descriptions that surround and condemn them. They can never, will never be able to own all the centuries of history that constitute Britishness, which is more than being 'born here'. But knowing that they are always on the periphery of class and culture, our children would find the segments of history acceptable to themselves and affirm, 'My forebears gave their souls, their spirit, their lives in the defence and reconstruction of this "green and pleasant land"'. The names of slave-owners survive in the names of banks, streets, museums full of plunder and the institutions of colonisation and economic castration.

Surely our descendants are entitled to say, with proviso, 'I call this place my home. Make what you like of my visibility. It is between yourself and your conscience.' A good dialogue to hold at this point of time and being.

Ferdinand Dennis

◆◆◆◆◆◆◆◆◆◆◆◆◆◆◆◆◆◆◆◆◆◆◆◆

Journeys without Maps

Ferdinand Dennis was a child-immigrant from Jamaica. His first book, *Behind the Frontlines: Journey into Afro-Britain*, was based on a journey through six English and Welsh cities and won the 1988 Martin Luther King Memorial Prize. Much of his work has explored the expressions of Africanness among African descendants. His most recent novel, *Duppy Conqueror*, is described by the *Guardian* as 'a landmark in British fiction'.

At the indeterminate age of eight I found myself aboard a ship called the *Montserrat* sailing away from Kingston Harbour and destined for Southampton, England, and then London where I would be reunited with my father. As the cloud-enwreathed mountains shrank, I clung to the railing of the ship and cried. Surrounded by my two brothers, sister and mother, I had no reason to shed tears but tears are seldom caused by reason. After Port au Spain, Caracas, and Valencia the ship docked at Southampton. My memories, thirty-odd years later, are of four children huddled around their mother. A cold, sharp wind tore through my thin cotton clothes and flesh, penetrating, it seemed, into the marrow of my bones; then the train ride to London through a night illuminated now and again by the lights of towns and cities; then reunion with my father. The acrid odour of paraffin, winter-dead trees and hedges, and the strange warmth of a duffel coat.

Much of those early years were lost in the trauma of arrival, exacerbated to an incalculable degree by the almost immediate breakdown of my parents' marriage. Within months my mother departed with my sister, leaving me and my two brothers in the care of my father. Physically dislocated, I was for many years also emotionally disoriented, confused and unhappy, grieving my mother's inexplicable absence, waiting for her to walk back through the door.

We lived in a three-storey terraced house in north Paddington, on the edge of the City of Westminster. Farther north, London changed and became more leafy, suburban. It was a community of immigrants from Nigeria, southern Europe and various parts of the Caribbean such as St Lucia, Dominica, Barbados, Guyana, Nevis. Most of the Caribbean folk worked hard and attended church regularly. I attended the local Church of England but in my mother's absence, religion and its many rituals ceased to play a part in my life. A small notorious minority kept blues dances in derelict houses and danced through weekend nights listening to melancholy music of lost, betrayed and fearful love. Within the boundaries of our neighbourhood I felt safe, protected. The women in particular, knowing of my mother's departure, were kindly and generous with their affection.

My father was a carpenter and held a passionate but essentially utilitarian belief in education. It was a means of social improvement along narrowly defined routes, usually connected with the construction industry. He was ambitious. He saw his three sons becoming surveyors or architects. The books he kept in the house reflected that ambition. Impenetrable and outdated tomes of unknown provenance on mechanics and mathematics sat on a shelf in the living room with two other works, the Bible and, much later, the *Kama Sutra*. We, my two brothers and I, were not forced to read, but encouraged to take education seriously by a man for whom idleness, indolence and a lack of ambition were punishable misdemeanours.

I had had a few years of Roman Catholic schooling, unusual

in a largely Protestant culture, and that too came to an end. My new school was called Wilberforce. Sometime in my secondary schooling the cloud began to lift. Playground fights at my London comprehensive, an austere archetypal 1960s building near Marble Arch, were frequent occurrences. All male, with pupils from the English working class and the Commonwealth, the older boys pounded the younger boys and rival gangs of football supporters – mostly Chelsea, Arsenal and Tottenham – avenged or celebrated their teams' victory or defeat the previous Saturday in running battles that mystified those of us who were new to England and the peculiarities of the English. For reasons now forgotten, at about the age of thirteen, I was involved in a playground fight. Prematurely ended by the teacher on duty, the outcome of that altercation was bloody and inconclusive.

Later that day I tried to give expression to a persisting swirl of emotions, an implacable agitation, in a piece of writing which aspired to some vague notion of poetry. The poem, long lost in my peripatetic life, concluded, 'You are now blind and I am now deaf, who won?' Its literary merit was probably worthless, but the exercise gave me such an immense feeling of satisfaction that I often returned to the solitary act of writing when over-whelmed by the impenetrable complexity of my situation. The act of writing would become a means of healing wounds acquired during my short lifetime, but it would also expose other, deeper wounds that were part of my legacy.

I began to withdraw from many of the activities that engaged my peers. I took to sketching the view from my bedroom window, a view of grey slated roofs, chimney stacks and sham-bolic gardens. I wrote portraits of the tenants, men and women drifting around London in search of a home. I recorded their idiosyncracies, their quarrels, their love affairs. I excavated and preserved in writing fragmented memories of the tropical island I had been taken from. Around the same time I discovered the wonders of the public library. There were three – redbricked, neo-gothic facades, all built in the late Victorian years – within walking distance of the house and as I progressed into my teens they became favourite haunts. They were peaceful, tranquil and yet full of adventures. The books I read were selected randomly, without any guidance, and consumed for sheer pleasure rather than any adolescent literary ambition. One day I chanced upon a collection titled *Nine African Short Stories*, by Doris Lessing. One story told of a White boy in South Africa who, roaming the veldt early one morning, thinks: 'I am sixteen and I can be anything I want in my life.'

I was not White, not yet sixteen, hadn't the vaguest idea what a veldt looked like, but that sentence had a profound impact on me. My empathy with the character flowed from the fact that I was doing a paper round at the time and was often abroad at an early hour of the morning when the musical rattle of milk floats was the most common sound in the still, quiet of the city. My father, who loved buildings, had impressed upon me the architectural greatness of London in Sunday morning car rides through the deserted city. The River Thames and its historical bridges, Park Lane, Buckingham Palace, Westminster Cathedral, Trafalgar Square were all short bus rides from home. Later I would see vast open expanses in Africa and understand better how space and the intoxicating scent of the morning could have prompted that grandiose thought in Lessing's character. London became my equivalent to Lessing's veldt. So I too began to say to myself 'I can be anything I want to be'.

I did not know what I wanted to be but knew with absolute certainty what I did not want to be. Thus began a protracted battle to avoid becoming what others wanted to make me. School encouraged us to leave as soon as possible – then fifteen – and take advantage of the numerous apprenticeships available in car mechanics, printing (much sought after) and other trades. None of those attracted me and I resented the crude attempts to direct me down channels that I had no interest in exploring. I had not shone at school but I believed that I could do better than their lowly estimation of my capability. With my father's support, I resisted their efforts to terminate my schooling and adopted the attitude that I was engaged in a form of rebellion. I started taking exams.

Some years later, I left school for a further education college in King's Cross to study A levels. There, I encountered more mature students, many of whom lived in Brixton and had experience of belonging to community political organisations, such as the Black Panthers. They formed the bedrock of the college's Black Student Society, which regularly invited guest speakers and performers. During my two years there I listened to speakers like Darcus Howe, Cecil Gutzmore, John La Rose and saw Linton Kwesi Johnson in performance with his band One Love. We held intense, lengthy discussions on the 'Black experience', swopped books like *Black Power* by Stokely Carmichael, *Seize the Time* by Bobby Seale and the *Autobiography of Malcolm X*, *Black Skin, White Mask* and *Wretched of the Earth* by Frantz Fanon and *Soul on Ice* by Eldridge Cleaver. These heady books gave me a language which helped to make sense of my situation which seemed to lack historical precedent and about which no books had been written.

This was something of a period of awakening for me. I began to describe myself as Black. I wore a black beret, black leather jacket and black corduroy trousers. My language was littered with phrases and words borrowed from other people's experiences. The African-Americans provided the most extensive vocabulary. It did not matter to me then that I had never known a situation of racial segregation, attended an all-Black school or lived in an all-Black neighbourhood. Somehow, I had journeyed from being a Jamaican child immigrant in Britain to becoming Black, a Black Briton, and carried within me all the alienation, anger and unease that such an identity, of necessity, must entail. I had become trapped in the Black-White duality. Mine was a negative identity, an identity defined in opposition to others, Whites. I was what Whites had made me, a victim of history, determined to infuse Blackness with something positive. An impossible task, of course. But I did not know that at the time.

Part of the problem for me was the lack of precedence. I

belong to a generation born in Britain or brought here as young children. Reaching an age when questions of identity are natural I could not turn to Caribbean writers for answers. The African-Americans provided some, though. But we often confuse likeness with sameness, similarity with identicality. Those people who continue to import African-American answers make that mistake. Indeed, in recent years I have often thought that just as the world is increasingly dominated by American culture, so the small population of people of African descent in Britain have become the victims of African-American cultural imperialism, mimicking styles and taking on concerns which sit uneasily in the British context, rather than engaging in the more difficult task of searching for a language to define the uniqueness of this situation.

I had continued scribbling in my father's house, writing stories about the tenants and neighbours, but did not take seriously the idea of becoming a writer. It seemed so vague, and being an immigrant, though I rejected my father's prescription for my future, I looked to occupations that would give me security and comfort. Literature remained a mere hobby, a secret pleasure which saw me read V. S. Naipaul's *Miguel Street*, Orlando Patterson's *Children of Sisyphus*, Ralph Ellison's *Invisible Man*, and all James Baldwin's works with only the ability to follow the narrative. I had no appreciation of the techniques used by those writers to create their effects.

A little over a decade after arriving in London, I went through another upheaval. I left home and London for university. From here on I was on my own, without a map and little idea of where I was heading. In between attending lectures, seminars and writing essays, I read voraciously. From the French existentialists, like Sartre and Camus, to more African-American writers, especially the poets, Langston Hughes and Countee Cullen, and now Latin American magic realists. By the end of my first degree such was my passion for literature that on several occasions I went out and bought new hardback novels by my favourite writers, then Gabriel Garcia Marquez and Naipaul.

While pursuing a postgraduate sociology degree, my interest in fiction came to occupy centre stage in a course that looked at Third World societies through their literature. The tutor had spent many years in Tanzania, Africa, and gave me the rudiments of critical reading. By the end of that course I knew that I would never become a sociologist. But how to become a writer?

A rough map came, as before, from the African-Americans. But this time, as I explored the works of writers from that part of the world, I discovered the works of a writer who became an inspirational example solely because we shared the same island of origin, Claude McKay. McKay had left Jamaica for the United States in his early twenties and lived a restless life in Harlem, Marseilles, London, Moscow and Morocco. This at a time when people from his background everywhere lived in a state of unfreedom. It seemed to me that if McKay could do it in such difficult circumstances, then I, the child of a far more enlightened and free age, could follow a similar path.

So I began consciously journeying towards becoming a writer. I tried turning my sketches of life in my father's house of tenants and growing up in an immigrant neighbourhood into short stories and discovered that while I had characters and locations I had no stories. I wrote a novel in six weeks – it was never published – and then started travelling. I went back to Jamaica for the first time and a few weeks after returning to London visited Nigeria. A year later, I went to Nigeria again and stayed for two years, lecturing in a Northern Nigerian University. It would be the last occasion I used the discipline I had learned at university to make my living.

The African experience was an important one; though I taught at the university, I also finished my formal education there. It destroyed my perception of myself as 'Black'. My colleagues at the Nigerian university came from all corners of that country and other parts of Africa. They were Yorubas, Ibos, Hausas, Ugandans, Ghanaians. They belonged to tribes, nations and religions. To describe myself as Black in a situation where most people shared my complexion was absurd. I had to rediscover and assert my Jamaicanness but qualify it with references to my London upbringing. I began to take pride in the diversity of my past, the cultural journeys I had made, which enabled me to mourn the death of John Lennon one Christmas and Bob Marley six months later, celebrate Gabriel Garcia Marquez winning the Nobel Prize for literature, and watch with passionate interest the marriage of Prince Charles and Diana Spencer on Nigerian television. I embraced the complexity of my being and decided to begin exploring that in writing. At the height of the Harmattan, in the cool nights of the rainy season, I wrote.

On returning to London this time, I threw myself into journalism as part of a consciously accelerated effort to become a writer. This was the London of the 1980s, the capital city of a nation wrestling with what it meant to be British with the death of empire. It was the decade when the Prime Minister Margaret Thatcher was engaged in attempting to put the Great back into Britain by bashing a banana republic in South America over a small British colony – The Falklands – and reviving the Victorian values believed to have made Britain great. It was the decade when Britain also began to recognise that it had to adjust to the presence of a large immigrant population from its former colonies. Inner city riots involving the alienated children of Caribbean settlers inspired by rastafarianism, a bizarre cult which mirrored the all-White Britishness project, and police forces riddled with racism, shook the establishment. Every major British institution began to seek ways of including a people who were British by birth and upbringing but whose collective identity seemed to have been forged by racism past and present, a people who were assimilated but not integrated.

Like all periods of change, confusion abounded. Some of those wishing to do good embarked on the road to hell and dragged others along with them. While the majority culture retreated into Whiteness and heritage and imaginary national homogeneity, a culture of anti-racism thrived, positing an equally imaginary racial homogeneity. Though the anti-racists meant well, they perpetuated the labelling of people as Black and attempted to include under that nomenclature every Briton who was experiencing real or imagined exclusion, from Irish to Chinese immigrants. The negativity implicit in the label informed a political project. Peoples of African-Caribbean origins were encouraged to believe that as they were of a certain shade, they were the victims of racism therefore their principal identity was Black. Being Black meant being radical, dread-locked, anti-establishment, belonging to the 'other' Britain united by a common experience of racism. There seemed to be a denial of the incredible diversity of the peoples defined as Black. The Afro-Caribbeans with their shattered cultures and Asians with whole cultures which enabled them to better with-stand the pressures of racism were lumped together. That we all carry within us a plurality of ever shifting and often conflicting identities, and all immigrants even more so, was considered a distraction from the anti-racist project. We were imprisoned in Black-White duality.

Against that cultural and political backdrop, I hustled for freelance work and jobs, I worked on short stories, another novel, and continued my catholic reading pleasure. Hemingway, Greene, Maugham, Faulkner, were consumed along with Alice Walker, Toni Morrison, Tony Cade Bambara and Olive Senior. Several short stories of mine were published, boosting my con-fidence. I finally finished a second novel during a period of unemployment, found an agent and then embarked on a brief career as a radio broadcaster. My first book, *Behind the Frontlines, a journey into Afro-Britain,* was published during this period and the publication of the novel, *The Sleepless Summer,* followed a year later. Both books, written out of what had gradually become a burning ambition, were however nothing more than starters. The craft of writing, the business of publishing, the great mystery of literary success remained to be pursued.

Whatever our endeavour, we need a measure of luck, the kiss of the capricious lady fortune. A measure of luck came my way some years after my first publication when I was invited to sit on the Arts Council of Britain's Literature advisory panel. I did not immediately recognise this invitation as good fortune. I had begun making a name for myself as a writer and broadcaster – something I had pursued to pay the rent – and was used to being invited to sit on committees. I accepted out of respect for the person who had recommended my name, Margaret Busby, and a sense of civic duty. Up until then I had sometimes seen writing as at best a compulsion and at worst a sickness. Suddenly I found myself seated around a long table with eminent figures from the world of letters all earnestly discussing the funding of literature and revealing in asides feelings and thoughts that I shared. My sense of civic duty gave way first to enlightenment born of the discovery of the myriad schemes and organisations for supporting aspiring writers, then to pleasure.

My time on the Literature Panel opened my eyes in other ways. I became aware of the danger, flowing from the desire to accommodate the African-Caribbean presence here, of formulating quasi-apartheid policies. Having discovered the pleasures of reading and writing before my racial awakening, I was alarmed to hear intelligent people speak of encouraging 'Black literature' and the birth of a 'new genre' called 'Black British fiction'. While it is certainly true that some British writers of African-Caribbean origin are concerned with race – there has, for example, been exploration of slavery in several works – the majority of writers who have emerged in recent years do not share that preoccupation. Victor Headley's *Yardie* – a good story, well written, poorly edited, but marketed with originality and panache – is probably the most successful book from this sudden growth in fiction from British writers with African-Caribbean antecedents. It is not about race, but about an illegal immigrant, a drugs dealer from Jamaica.

Works like *Yardie* are not great fiction, but they represent an important development. For much of this century writers of African ancestry have explored lives constrained by the narrow and iniquitous fact of race. As we approach the millennium, there has been a noticeable diversity in the themes explored by such writers: love, the family, religion, art – themes that most writers have always taken for granted. I welcome this departure and look forward to reading novels where the character's colour is secondary to the story. Whether the conservative, hidebound publishing establishment will treat such works with the seriousness they deserve is of course another matter.

Having recently entered my forties, my concern now is to juggle generating an income with writing. The long-term goal is, of course, to make a living from writing. Some years ago, I abandoned journalism and broadcasting for a while and tried teaching creative writing at an adult education institute, but found this so frustrating that I soon gave it up. The paucity of resources, the lack of an intellectual and artistic community in the institute made conditions intolerable. I felt I had fallen and the only way to rise was to fall further into unemployment which would give me back my days, especially the precious morning hours when dreams are best pursued. I took that option.

Since then I have continued to write full-time. It's a rewarding but unprofitable occupation. Yet I am now more than ever aware of the importance of this venture. To chronicle lives and experiences that might otherwise be forgotten because they are marginal, to assert a presence so often overlooked in the past. On wet, melancholy days, sitting at my desk, staring out onto Finsbury Park, I bolster my mood by reminding myself that I have chosen what I want to be. It has been a long, slow journey and I have probably dallied too long at particularly beautiful sights, taken one or two too many digressions, invited disasters – all inevitable on a journey without a map – but it remains a fascinating challenge. Heaven knows what I would do with myself if I should ever arrive!

John Figueroa
✦✦✦✦✦✦✦✦✦✦✦✦✦✦✦✦✦✦✦✦

Becoming a Caribbean Man

John Figueroa, who passed away while this anthology was being
prepared, belonged to the generation of writers who put
Caribbean literature on the map. An academic and poet, he was a
regular contributor to *Bim*, the famous 1950s Caribbean literary
magazine, and one of the earliest contributors to the pioneering
BBC World Service programme *Caribbean Voices*. His two-volume
anthology of Caribbean poetry remains the best of its kind.

One is often asked to express an opinion on the effect on
one's writing of coming to England and living in it. First
of all, I must stress that I came to the United Kingdom in 1946
before the big immigration of Jamaicans and other West Indians
to this country. Moreover, I had been at college in the USA in
Worcester, Massachusetts, from 1938–42. In those 'bad old days'
one could see in New York boarding houses the sign 'Vacancies
– No Jews, No Coloureds'. Sometimes, to make the exclusion
perfect was added 'No Dogs'.

I imagine that among writers who are expressing an opinion
on the question I have noted above I must be one of the oldest,
and also one of the first, who came to work and live in England.

I would say, without going too deeply into the unconscious
and all that, I think that my visit to the UK in 1946, and my
living here until 1953–54, had two major effects on me. One, it
taught me an awful lot about the Caribbean, and, in fact, made

it easy for me to become *'un hombre del Caribe'*. The second
effect it had on me was to give me a certain amount of self
belief. Both of these results were very much helped by my first
visit to the BBC, and to my subsequent working for it. The other
agency, if I may put it that way, was playing regular cricket for
the West Indies Wanderers, a team managed by Kenneth Ablack
(Trinidad), Learie Constantine (Trinidad) and Bertie Clarke
(Barbados), who also captained the team. I am calling upon
extracts from my *Memoirs* to throw light on the role of the BBC
and the West Indies Wanderers.

As soon as I settled in London I called on John Grenfell
Williams, then Head of Overseas Broadcasting. I had brought a
letter of introduction to him from Cedric Lindo of Jamaica, who,
with his wife, acted as BBC agent in the West Indies.

Grenfell Williams had left South Africa because he and a
friend had published a novel called *I am Black but Beautiful*. This
quotation from the Song of Songs did not endear him to the
authorities and I believe that he had to leave the country.

I walked to John Grenfell Williams' office, which was at 200
Oxford Street, where the recording studios were many metres
below the ground to protect them from the German bombing.
He gave me a rather warmer welcome than I expected from
such a high officer in the BBC and he took me into a room near
to his where the West Indies section worked, with the exception
of Henry Swanzy. He introduced me as the man who had written
'that short story, *Do you appreciate music?*' and I was, I fear,
lionised. Henry was called in and congratulated me on the
short story. He explained that it was the first thing that he
had broadcast on *Caribbean Voices* when he had taken over the
programme. He invited me to submit any other short stories or
poetry 'I might have in my briefcase'.

This welcome and attitude contrasted greatly with the reception which I and my verse had received at home. To quote but
one critic, Orford St John: 'It is no discourtesy to the work of T.
S. Eliot to say that he gave birth to a generation of vipers. John
Figueroa is unfortunately among the offenders.' ('Perspective

on *Focus'*, p 83). Other critics felt the same way. Kenneth Ramchand of Trinidad included in his list of publications of Jamaican poetry the collection which Archie Lindo published about the same time as my *Blue Mountain Peak*. But he omitted mine. Even long after, when an anthology was made up by Cedric Lindo and Robert Verity to celebrate the Federation, only one of my poems was included.

Henry Swanzy gave me an appointment to come back to see him, and I submitted some of my better poems. We made up a programme and from that time I was a regular broadcaster on his programme *Caribbean Voices*.

I was offered work from time to time by the other people in the Caribbean section – E. R. Edmett, Ken Ablack, who had flown in the RAF – and others. I enjoyed most of all my work with Henry. I had a clear voice suitable to the short waves, and I had broadcast a bit when I was at college. But Henry taught me a great deal about pausing and emphasis and that kind of thing. I was to work for him for quite a few years, until I noticed that something was going wrong.

Henry had insisted on paying us the going rate for work on his programme, and I am sure that the local branch of Equity, the artists' union, was complaining that we were mere amateurs and were being paid the going rate. But beside the pressure of Equity I was to discover long after another cause for my being used less often as a reader of poetry. I found this in copies of letters written to the BBC's *Caribbean Voices*. Cedric Lindo and his wife urged that Henry Swanzy should take me off the reading of poetry. Swanzy wrote a stout letter in my defence saying I was one of the best readers of poetry he had met. But the Lindos insisted. Further, George Lamming, with his wonderful reading voice, had come to England with a letter of recommendation from the one and only Frank Collymore, who was the greatly respected editor in Barbados of *Bim*, and George was given some of the poetry reading. However, I was not denied other broadcasting opportunities with the very much needed fees, for Edmett and others started to use me regularly in the rest of the

Caribbean section – I suspect that this was by agreement with Henry Swanzy and John Grenfell Williams. I also did a special programme on poetry for Schools Broadcasting which was used for many years.

Henry Swanzy was not alone in his opinion of my ability to read poetry for at the exact same time that the Lindos were complaining George Lamming and I were giving public readings in many parts of London. This was to lead to a BBC Third Programme poetry reading done by George and myself and by the producer of Dylan Thomas' *Under Milk Wood*.

These readings led to my being asked by the New York firm of Caedmon to produce a record called 'Caribbean Writers Reading Their Own Work' which was eventually turned into a cassette.

The explanation for the really vicious attack that the Lindos made on my reading is very difficult to understand – maybe they just didn't like how I read poetry, but there was more to it than that because when Mr Bunting came over as manager of the Jamaican men's team to the 1948 Olympics, Mrs Lindo kept writing to Swanzy and asking him why he had not used Bunting who she said was such an excellent reader of poetry. Mr Bunting was head of Wolmers Boys' School in Jamaica – he was very fond of poetry and wrote a bit himself. But he was a Wordsworthian, and read with a very sweet and very English voice. I suspect that Mrs Lindo thought that was the only voice, even for Caribbean poems. But Henry Swanzy, and no doubt I, being a much smaller character than he, earned very great dislike because George Lamming's book *In the Castle of My Skin* (which I proofread) had been very much praised by London critics and the BBC, whereas Roger Mais of Jamaica could not get a review in London. Mrs Lindo was very annoyed about this and said that Lamming's book was very boring and she wasn't surprised about this as a Barbadian lady had told her that Lamming himself was very boring. She also noted that *Newsweek* magazine had given him a very favourable notice. She added, however, 'Not that I think that *Newsweek* knows much about novels!'

I was very sorry that when I last went to Jamaica and gave six open seminars on Caribbean Voices, Cedric Lindo did not turn up – unfortunately Mrs Lindo had died some time ago. I had really wished to discuss with him his attack on me. Unfortunately he has subsequently died, and I can't gain any direct personal insight into what the matter was.

I introduced George Campbell's poems to Henry Swanzy. Through me Carmen Manley introduced M. G. Smith's poems. I thought that the latter was a better poet than Campbell but Campbell was our first recently published poet in Jamaica and as a protégé of Edna Manley he was much praised. Unfortunately I discovered at the recent memorial service for M. G. Smith that he had been denying that he had ever written poetry and did not wish any of it to be read at his memorial. He had become a very distinguished anthropologist and became very worried, I understand, that his poetry betrayed an interest in mysticism and spirituality which as he grew older he had rid himself of.

So when I got cut down on the Swanzy programmes I was used by the West Indian section for news reading, and especially for sports broadcasting, including the 1948 Olympic Games in which little Jamaica did very well, and signalled that through Wint, MacKinley and others they were soon to be the world-beating 400 metres relay team.

It will be understood from what I have said above why the BBC work gave me a certain belief in myself and in my writing and why, sometimes to some people's astonishment, I have always praised Henry Swanzy highly. The whole of Caribbean literature owed him a great debt while he was running the programme, from 1946 to 1955. In fact the *Times Literary Supplement* said that at that time West Indian writers freely acknowledged their debt to the BBC, both financial and aesthetic. Anne Walmsley points out in her book on the Caribbean Artists' Movement the value of Swanzy's pioneering editorship, as do E. K. Braithwaite and Vidia Naipaul. I do not know why

many people at the University of the West Indies, who should
know better, do not like Swanzy's extremely good work in this
direction to be acknowledged.

I should have mentioned that he had been asked to take over
the programme from Una Marson, the Jamaican woman, who
had been a distinguished worker in the League of Coloured
People and who had started the programme *Caribbean Voices*.
She had become suddenly ill and it was at that time that Swanzy
was asked to take it over. Her work did not meet one of
Swanzy's main criteria which was that the writing he wanted
to publish should be particularly Caribbean, and not the general
sort of thing which any good poet could write. I myself had
many arguments about this, for it seemed to limit Caribbean
writers too much. But by the time he gave up to go to West
Africa he had broadcast at least 150 Caribbean writers and given
them encouragement as well as criticism. These included, among
others, Derek Walcott, Louise Bennett, Eric Roach, Sam Selvon
and Ian McDonald (on one occasion he had even been to Paris
to try to collect some of the most distinguished writing of the
French Caribbean).

This meant that reading on the programme, and taking part
in the critical discussions which we held on the work, introduced
me not only to Caribbean critics but also to a large body of
Caribbean writing. My work on the programme therefore prepared me to realise that there was much more to the Caribbean
than Jamaica; it also gave me great confidence in my reading
and in my ability to discuss and criticise literature, a confidence
which would have been gladly undermined by the Lindos, and
some other Jamaicans, who apparently hate to see a fellow
Jamaican doing well in London.

As I have said above, the other influence on my realising
how large the Caribbean was, and how many different cultures
existed – even without taking into account Puerto Rico, and the
Republica Dominicana and the French-speaking islands – was
my playing regularly for the West Indies Wanderers of London.
Beside the players whom I have already mentioned we regularly

had team-mates from Barbados, Grenada, Guyana etc. From time to time we had some of the greats who played in the North of England to join us. These included Weeks and even George Headley. One memorable occasion was the joining of our team by Snuffie Brown of Guyana who, even at an advanced age, dropped every ball of every over just on the right spot.

In mentioning New York at the beginning of this piece I hinted at the racial prejudice against Jews and Blacks. The prejudice that I mostly met in discussions with my colleagues at the BBC and elsewhere was that I was often written off as a scion of some rich planter family. My critics soon dropped this attitude when they discovered that my paternal grandfather had come from Panama to Jamaica, probably as a political refugee when it was still part of Colombia, and that my maternal grandfather had rowed a boat with his brothers and cousins from Cuba to the east end of Jamaica. His family had decided to leave Cuba after his father had been executed for supporting José Marti.

The xenophobic prejudice against the lesser breed without the law was, of course, always present in the UK. One worker at the BBC found it difficult to rent a flat because the landlord did not wish either Coloureds or Roman Catholics. But the real powerful and panic prejudice was to come later when the large and powerful 'Mother Country' became afraid of being overrun by three or four shipfuls of its children from the Caribbean.

David Dabydeen

❖❖❖❖❖❖❖❖❖❖❖❖❖❖❖❖

West Indian Writers in Britain

David Dabydeen belongs to the younger generation of writers who
made the crossing from the Caribbean. Of Indo-Guyanese ancestry,
he is an internationally renowned poet, novelist, essayist and is
director of the Caribbean Studies Centre in Warwick University.
His non-fiction work includes an incisive study of Hogarth's
depiction of Africans in London, and the history of Indian
migration to the Caribbean.

Many people today, worldwide, remember exactly what
they were doing when John F. Kennedy was assassinated
in Dallas. I remember distinctly where I was when I first read
my first West Indian novel, Naipaul's *Miguel Street*. I was in
our house in New Amsterdam, British Guyana. I was eleven.
Although the house was normally crowded (there were nine of
us at the time) I remember a solitude in which Naipaul's novel
was the sole presence. And the overwhelming pleasure I felt in
the presence of the novel was due to a recognition of myself
and my surroundings, as if for the first time. Here were characters who behaved and spoke like our own people, and they
were in the pages of a book which our schoolteacher had
instructed the class to read: a book therefore that had authority.
Before *Miguel Street* there were dozens of Nancy Drew and
Hardy Boys novels, comic books, Aesop, Charles Lamb's *Tales
from Shakespeare*, children's versions of Greek and Roman myths,

Ladybird histories of great scientists, artists, explorers and generals (for our humble public library was stocked with a fine sample of English and American publications). Like other children, I read as much as I could: there was no television in the country, and the library occupied as central a place in childhood as the cricket field and the cinema. The books from England and America were enchanting, but it was the enchantment of a world outside of Guyana, an immeasurably bigger and more heroic world which I knew – as colonial children did – I would encounter one day as an emigrant or student. The experience of reading Naipaul was entirely different. It was about me – all of us – struggling to achieve, but failing in sad and comic ways. The failure was not dismal – like the Africans in the Tarzan films – but poignant, showing us to be people of ambition and humility. We were small people, but we had human qualities.

Later in life, I can see incipient, if not open, contempt in *Miguel Street* for the West Indian character, but as a boy, I felt only pathos, possibly because the pathos of the novel was not unlike that in the Bombay film melodramas which Indo-Guyanese grew up on. The Bombay films were also about small people mired in poverty and adversity, hustling to survive or to triumph over their circumstances by marrying the rich lawyer's daughter or into the upper castes, or gaining a place at university and a subsequent powerful profession.

The Indian dimension to Naipaul's writing and character has stayed with me, inevitably, since I am of Indian origin. The novels I've written so far are forms of wrestling with Naipaul, the revered and despised Indian, the revered and despised father figure. My childhood in Guyana was marked by a sense of Indian inferiority. We had a measure of political power, but in a fragile way. Most of us were subsistence farmers. The rich Indian businessmen and professionals were as alien to us as the urbane and sophisticated Afro-Guyanese who seemed to run the country. The politicians were mostly Black, and in our illiteracy we were vulnerable to their superior knowledge of the

Law as well as to their superior physical build. Apart from politically inspired race riots in the early 1960s, rarely did Black people behave badly towards us. Quite the opposite: I (and many of my generation in New Amsterdam, of differing ethnic groups) owe my early educational ambitions to one Mr Spencer, a local Afro-Guyanese teacher who in his day was celebrated for his outstanding care of his pupils. But the Spencers of the world seemed unusual: although there was little or no overt violence done to us, we lived in a mood of subdued fear of our Black neighbours and fellow citizens, who outnumbered us considerably in New Amsterdam.

These were the impressions of boyhood – a sense of actual or imagined bullying by Black people – which account for the prominence of Indians like the politician Cheddi Jagan and the cricketer Rohan Kanhai in my mind. They were powerful men who were acknowledged leaders in their fields. So was Naipaul, the writer of a book which was a classroom set text.

The subsequent wrestling with Naipaul is partly due to my desire to explore what I most revere and despise in the Indo-Caribbean. In my first novel, *The Intended*, I explore Black-Indian tensions in Guyana and in Britain, in the person of an unnamed Indo-Guyanese character who vacillates between self-contempt and outrage at Black failure. Halfway through the novel I realised that it was an imagined biography (and possibly, travesty) of a young 'Naipaul' wanting the values of Oxford which are set against a valueless Black world. In the second novel, *Disappearance*, a Naipaulian rationality, detachment and ironic manner are represented in the figure of the engineer. In the latest novel, *Counting House*, the central character is called Vidia, and I try to understand his sense of sexual inability as well as his obsession with money. Needless to say, all these characters may well be versions of myself rather than of Naipaul, and I will happily engage with any allegation that I am merely 'wearing the mask of Naipaul' to secrete my own failings and excesses. The point I wish to make, however, is that Naipaul has had a profound and direct impact on West Indian writers of my generation. We no longer 'write back' to Conrad and Defoe, but to the likes of Naipaul, and in so doing, we create a sense of a living literary tradition which is distinctly West Indian. Those who came in the boats in the 1940s onwards, equipped with little but their imaginations, 'fathered' West Indian literature and 'fathered' works by subsequent generations. The (en)gendering of the literature is now being examined by scholars like Evelyn O'Callaghan, Carolyn Cooper and Ramabai Espinet, who point to our ignorance of the seminal works of Una Marson, Rajkumari Singh, and Louise Bennett. The re-issuing of women's writings introduces the contemporary West Indian writer to an even more varied body of ancestral voices.

Ancestral voices can however be tyrannical. Selvon and Harris may have written in the freedom of knowing that they came from largely unrecorded backgrounds. The landscape and the people of the West Indies were there to be written about almost for the first time. This sense of freedom would have held certain terrors, but what terror can compare to that I, and others, face today: the terror of the genius of the ancestral voices? They have mapped out the territory with such awesome talent that what is there left for me to say? I cannot write about the sea without reference to Walcott. I cannot write about the Guyanese rainforest without reference to Wilson Harris. I cannot write about an Indian childhood, or about peasantry, without reference to Sam Selvon. Tradition is a splendid idea, but it can stifle individual talent.

My personal ambition is to try to live up to the literary standards set by the earlier writers. 'Audience' for me does not reside in the criticisms of British readers, though I am grateful for these, shamelessly so when the responses are positive. I really don't mind being a victim of any British appetite for the exotic, if it means that I can get some royalties here and there. As to the British guilt for the Empire which translates into book buying and prize giving, I'll gladly jostle in the queue for handouts and reparations. (I've even contemplated writing a sombre novel on slavery to cash in on White angst.) I can only recognise myself as a 'proper' writer, however, when Harris or Walcott or Braithwaite or Naipaul have a kind and genuine word to say about anything I have published. I live in dread of their critical utterances.

In other words, one is not just conscious of previous Caribbean literature, but also the processes by which it came about, and my position in it.

In 1992, on the 500th Anniversary of Christopher Columbus' adventure in the West Indies, Derek Walcott was awarded the Nobel Prize for Literature. St Lucia is a dot on the world's map. Without modern navigational technology, the British Airways pilot could so easily miss the island and fly on to the continent of South America. Columbus himself had taken the wrong turnings and instead of reaching his expected destination of India, he had arrived at another place, which he titled West India, christening its natives Indians.

As the plane descends to land in St Lucia you see a few fields of scrawny sugarcane, some untidy allotments, goats in untended fields, and patches of housing. Naipaulian images of an unfinished society come to mind, but these are qualified when you recall the creativity of the St Lucian, a creativity that can be measured by the fact that in the last forty years, St Lucia has given the world two Nobel Prize winners. In the 1960s Arthur Lewis was given the Prize for Economics: Imagine winning the Nobel Prize for Economics coming from a country with no economy to speak of, indeed, when whatever economy you inhabited was in total control and possession of the British, since you were of colonial status. Derek Walcott was the second St Lucian to be honoured by the world, and the dot of his island had the powerful status of a full stop at the end of a sentence. It gave definition to a sentence by closing it, in this case the Columbian phase or phrase of our existence which sentenced indigenous peoples to extermination, but which also saw the survival, adaptation and creative transformation of African and Asian cultures in the region, in spite of three centuries of slavery and indentureship. Walcott once said that, at the beginning of his poetic career, he couldn't mention the word 'mango' in his poetry for fear of confusing and alienating English publisher and English reader alike. By 1992, Walcott had been able to name his landscape and define the culture of the region.

Walcott's *Omeros* is dedicated to 'shipmates in the craft', the craft not being only the craft of poetry but also the slave and coolie boats which brought us to the Caribbean from the days of Elizabeth I, and eventually landed us in England in the days of Elizabeth II. After the Second World War, West Indians were recruited to Britain to help rebuild its fabric, to work in hospitals, factories and railway and bus depots. Among the mass of workers arriving on the boats were a few prospective writers, people of Walcott's generation. There were James Berry and Edward Braithwaite, Sam Selvon and George Lamming, Andrew Salkey and Michael Anthony, Stuart Hall and V. S. Naipaul, Jan Carew and Wilson Harris, an all-male line-up. These early writers, coming in different boats and from different islands, shared Walcott's passion to name self and to name landscape. The Trinidadian Sam Selvon said that 'I believe that the West Indian novelist had, among his major responsibilities, that of making his country and his people known accurately to the rest of the world' (the 'rest of the world' in his day being, of course, England). Roger Mais, a Jamaican novelist, wrote that his purpose in writing was to reveal something of 'the dreadful conditions of the Jamaican working classes'. His contemporary Vic Reid said that his project was to describe 'the kindliness, humour and beauty of my people'. When V. S. Naipaul began to publish, C. L. R. James wrote to him to congratulate him for 'showing the English what stuff we are made of'.

Literary efforts at self-definition and self-description coincided with agitation for Independence and decolonisation. Some writers like Martin Carter and Roger Mais were jailed in the Caribbean for opposition to Britain, and their poetry and fiction were nourished by political and prison experiences. Others, like C. L. R. James, wrote fiction, history and political philosophy, and worked closely with up and coming anti-colonial politicians like Jomo Kenyatta and Kwame Nkrumah for 'the liquidation of colonialism and imperialism'. The few West Indian cultural organisations that sprung up in Britain in the 1950s had political affiliations. James Berry, secretary of the African and Caribbean Social and Cultural Centre in Paddington, said that his group 'could not help being political'. Norman Manley, a leader of the Jamaican Independence movement, was one of several visiting speakers. 'Everybody who came over who was important, came and talked.' Cultural groups such as Berry's, whilst organising poetry writing workshops and the like, also issued political leaflets or participated in letter-writing campaigns to British Parliamentarians.

Most of the writers who emerged in the 1950s however had no direct personal involvement in political movements. They came to write poetry and fiction, not political tracts. They confessed a passionate and obsessive ambition to write works of the imagination, none more so than the Guyanese Edgar Mittleholzer. Mittleholzer uses the language of war in describing his efforts to write and to be published:

> In my imagination the whole thing had taken on the flavour of a military campaign. I was a general at the head of an army, and the objectives were clearly defined. The enemy was Life-cum-editors-and-publishers-in-London. I must hurl the whole weight of my war-machine against their defences, infiltrate here, infiltrate there, and then, in one big offensive, batter away at the inner fortifications until victory was achieved. The acceptance of a short short-story by a weekly paper would constitute a mere infiltration; the same would apply to an article. But a full-length story accepted by one of the monthly magazines, like *The Strand*, *Pearson's* or *The Royal*, would be a major breakthrough. Final victory would be represented by the acceptance of a novel by a publisher.

Mittleholzer wrote furiously and copiously, and posted from British Guiana several stories to English magazines, only to receive rejection slips and the return of his manuscripts under separate cover. The more he was repulsed, the more fanatical he became, penning stories for speedy despatch to the metropolis:

> Every time I looked in the newspaper and saw that a ship was due from England, I had to steel myself for an enemy onslaught. When I heard the postman dismount from his bicycle at the gateway, I knew it was Zero Hour. The bulky envelopes meant another repulse. Disheartening, but that was war. Attack again. Back went the manuscripts to other editors. Sometimes three or four went off at the same time, for I never stopped writing in the intervals of waiting to hear about those dispatched. No one guessed what a grim struggle was being waged. I presented a blank face to the outside world. I went to ice-cream matinees . . . and danced as though I were a carefree young man not yet settled in any special occupation. Only I could hear the artillery booming in the background, sometimes drowning out the wailing of the saxophone and the cling-clang of the piano.

Mittleholzer had to leave Guyana and travel to England to fulfil his ambition for a writing career. In the colonies there were no publishing houses or distribution systems. The few magazines that existed – magazines like *Bim* in Barbados, started in 1942, or *Kyk-over-al* in Guyana, started in 1945 – had scant readership, and paid nothing to contributors. Their quality was also uneven. Mittleholzer says bluntly, 'the local papers were of no interest to me so far as my main objective was concerned. Their standards were too low.' To be a writer you had to be validated by the centre, by being on the lists of a London publisher. To remain in the Caribbean was to languish in obscurity, and indeed to court self-annihilation. Sam Selvon says he could easily have dissipated his life in beach-parties, rum-drinking and middle-class flirtations:

> I went to London because I was becoming convinced that, had I stayed in Trinidad, I would have succumbed to the apathy which lured people into accepting their situation and social and

cultural circumstances. I wanted to confront the challenge of mainstream culture, or what had been presented to me as such at school. I needed not only the intellectual stimulation but the possibility of being published, heard; the possibility of making a living by writing as I did for the BBC. Only in London did my life find its purpose.

Finally it has to be said too that the writer in the West Indies was seen to be a kind of lunatic, one with no prospects of a decent house, a decent marriage and a decent situation in society. Why did one want to write when the thing to do was to become a lawyer or doctor or civil servant? V. S. Naipaul's character, B. Wordsworth in the novel *Miguel Street*, is a tragic-comic portrait of a would-be writer. B. Wordsworth – 'B' stands for 'Black' – is seen as an idler and an eccentric, one who will get nowhere with his life because of his unworldly literary ambitions. In any case, being Black, Trinidadian society automatically believe him to be lacking in talent; his ambitions therefore are seen to be even more ludicrous. He is doomed to rejection and penury:

> He pulled out a printed sheet from his hip-pocket and said, 'On this paper is the greatest poem about mothers and I am going to sell it to you at a bargain price. For four cents.'
>
> I went inside and I said, 'Ma, you want to buy a poetry for four cents?'
>
> My mother said, 'Tell that blasted man to haul his tail away from my yard, you hear.'
>
> I said to B. Wordsworth, 'My mother say she ain't have four cents.'
>
> B. Wordsworth said, 'It is the poet's tragedy.'

In addition, Naipaul is saying that B. Wordsworth, by remaining in Trinidad, is doomed to mimicry. The master-script is English, and the colonial writer is shackled to it, perceiving and describing his tropical, equatorial landscape in English romanticist images – of vales and meadows, rills and purling streams. Colonial brainwashing – the processes by which the Aethopian is washed white – means that only such images are acceptable to the Trinidadian reader as authoritative, as 'proper' literature. To find a native voice, the would-be writer has to emigrate away from colonial expectations.

And so the writers boarded the *SS Windrush* and later boats, equipped with little except fierce ambition, individual talent and, in the case of Sam Selvon and George Lamming, a shared 'Imperial' typewriter. Both Selvon and Lamming had had some literary experience: Selvon was a sub-editor of the *Trinidad Guardian*'s magazine supplement, and Lamming had acted as an agent for the Barbadian cultural journal *Bim*. Both were in the process of writing their first novels, and the boat trip to England allowed both some time to continue their work. Selvon talks of how Lamming would come to his cabin to borrow his typewriter, which he lent him reluctantly. Lamming would then conveniently forget to return the typewriter, or else would lock himself in his cabin and refuse to come out. Selvon would curse him in vivid Caribbean language and threaten to break down the door and choke him. The squabbling over the typewriter continued when they arrived in London and shared accommodation in a men's hostel, until Lamming bought his own second-hand machine. Ten years after the journey, Lamming wrote lyrically about Selvon's boat-novel, depicting him as a solitary, romanticist figure:

> Selvon and I, like members of some secret society were always together. But this comradeship turned to a strange reticence during the last few days of the journey. Sam had taken to walking alone in the more remote parts of the ship. Sometimes he would be seen working in odd corners: a small grey typewriter on his knees and long black locks of hair fallen forward, almost screening him from view. He would go up on the deck if no one was there. He would take refuge in the dormitory whenever it was empty.

Note the detailed recollection of the typewriter as being small and grey. The truth was probably that Selvon was not seeking the solitude of poets but merely trying to put distance between himself and Lamming.

Such then, were the humble origins of two outstanding seminal Caribbean novels, George Lamming's *In the Castle of my Skin*, published by Michael Joseph in 1953, and Sam Selvon's *A Brighter Sun*, published the year before by Alan Wingate.

Anne Walmsley, in her comprehensive study of the Caribbean Artists' Movement in Britain between 1966 and 1972, writes that:

> would-be writers arriving in Britain from the Caribbean in the 1950s found a range of opportunities and encouragement open to them, especially if they lived in London. Book publishing was experiencing somewhat of a post-war boom; small, young publishing houses were eager to bring out work by fresh, vigorous new voices from far corners of the Commonwealth, especially those who used English with the fluency, individuality and verve of West Indians. Publishers found a ready market for books about these writers' tropical home environment and society, despite their containing much implicit, and, especially in the work of Lamming, explicit criticism of colonialism. Books which reflected the new phenomenon of West Indians making their home in London also found an audience.

Sam Selvon himself spoke of the 'wonderment and accolade that greeted the boom of Caribbean literature and art in Britain in the early fifties.' Undoubtedly there is much truth in such statements. Between 1952 and 1958, Selvon, Lamming, John Hearne, Mittleholzer, Naipaul and Andrew Salkey published between them twenty novels, so we can assume that their publishers found sales to be satisfactory. Lamming won the Somerset Maugham Award in 1957 and Naipaul won it in 1959. Naipaul had also received, in 1957, the John Llewellyn Rhys Memorial Prize. Andrew Salkey received the Thomas Helmore Prize in 1955 and Sam Selvon was given a travelling scholarship by the

Society of Authors in 1958. Such honours are a measure of the favourable reception accorded to West Indian writers in the 1950s, though it has to be said that the experience of the mass of West Indians was very different: anti-black riots in 1953, and racial disturbances throughout the fifties, made the West Indian feel decidedly unwelcome in Britain.

The BBC's *Caribbean Voices* programme was the main platform for readings by West Indian writers and for discussion of their work. Being on the programme signified that the writer had arrived, and this sense of arrival was consolidated by the receipt of a BBC cheque for one's literary contribution. Sam Selvon talks of being awed by his first BBC cheque. The cheque, he says, was printed on thick textured paper which gave it imperial authority, and it was made out, not in plebeian pounds sterling but in gentlemanly guineas. Although the irony of being paid in currency, the title of which derived from the slave trade, was not lost on writers like Lamming and Selvon, the descendants of slaves, nevertheless they received it gladly. Selvon confesses to being dead broke, but carrying his cheque around for days before cashing it, so as to experience the privilege of being a writer, one so designated and anointed by the BBC.

Caribbean Voices however was aimed at a West Indian audience in the West Indies, and it is doubtful whether it made any significant impact on promoting Caribbean writing among a British readership. The programme after all was broadcast from London on a Sunday evening, at 23.15 GMT, when only the unemployed or insomniac were awake in Britain, the rest of the population retiring early in preparation for Monday morning work. The timing of the broadcast was solely because the West Indies were some eight hours behind GMT. It was the British newspaper and magazine which brought West Indian literature to the attention of the British, not the BBC's *Caribbean Voices* programme. All the major journals – *The Times, Times Literary Supplement, Manchester Guardian, Spectator, New Statesman* and *London Magazine* – reviewed West Indian writing on an immediate and regular basis. American journals readily available in Britain, like the *New York Times Book Review* and the *New Yorker*, also gave coverage to the emerging literature.

The most sensitive and intelligent of the British reviewers was undoubtedly Francis Wyndham, the distinguished editor, critic and prose writer. Wyndham reviewed regularly for the leading literary periodicals, and later became editor of *Queen* magazine and assistant editor of the *Sunday Times* magazine. He was instrumental in re-discovering Jean Rhys, who had totally disappeared from the British literary scene, and promoting a reassessment of her work. His championing of the technical genius of Jean Rhys is his greatest contribution to the appreciation of West Indian Literature. His reviews avoided the pitfalls of exotica and newness, drawing attention instead to the varied formal qualities of the writing. Take, for example, his review of Sam Selvon's collection of short stories, *Ways of Sunlight* (*The Times*, April 1953):

> The reviewer of novels is always, and sometimes rather desperately, on the look-out for anything which might be called a 'trend': it was, for example, a purely journalistic expedient which saddled the 'redbrick' writers with an inaccurate label and an unintended social significance. Can something be made of the fact that many of the most interesting post-war French books are by North Africans, while in the English literary scene of the fifties West Indian writers play an increasingly prominent part? Something, perhaps, about colonial vigour providing a necessary stimulus to decadent metropolitan culture? Better not try; even to refer to a West Indian 'school' is misleading, as the only merit these writers share is their independence of each other, an artistic variety which reflects the radical variety of their islands' populations. A school implies the existence of a master, here we have a collection of prefects, catholic enough to include the over-wrought eroticism of Edgar Mittleholzer, the Maugham-like narrative efficiency of John Hearne, the deceptive simplicity of V. S. Naipaul's ironic comedies, the rich, poetic loquacity of George Lamming, the limpid lyricism of Samuel Selvon.

David Dabydeen

He does not praise Selvon in a patronising way. Indeed he states boldly that 'Selvon's talent is not ideally suited to the novel' but to the short story. When he does speak highly of Selvon he does so with intelligence and restraint, again drawing attention to the writing as *writing*, rather than as Black exotica: 'Those told in dialect have an irresistible charm, owing as much to the author's technical subtlety as to the unfamiliar delights of the language.' Today's critics, motivated by race/class/or gender agendas, who treat literature as mere illustration of sociology, who promote or damn so-called 'Black' or 'Third-World' literature on ideological content, would find Wyndham's emphasis on *quality* and *form* to be rather quaint and colonial. Since all authors are dead or redundant, according to prevailing theory, such critics would dismiss as irrelevant the fact that writers like Selvon were in agreement with Wyndham's approach. Selvon resented reviews that relished his so-called 'primitive' and 'innocent' dialect, not appreciating the extraordinary effort he made as a writer to *conceal* the artfulness of his Creole so as to make it appear naturalistic. Later in life, Selvon wrote persuasively of the ways in which he shaped and transformed Creole to make it both lyrical and lucid to the English ear. He wanted to be appreciated as a language-alchemist, and for the Creolisation of the form of the English novel.

Compared to Francis Wyndham, most early reviews were riddled with errors or motivated by ideology. Maurice Richardson's review of Selvon's novel *An Island in a World* (1955) in the *New Statesman* (23 April 1955) gets Selvon's Indian ancestry completely wrong by stating, with utter and authoritative assurance, that Indo-Caribbeans are of Malayan origin. This, at best, betrays intellectual laziness on the part of Richardson; at worst an imperial mind that cannot discriminate between various subject peoples. Richardson is condescending about the anti-colonial mood of the novel: 'Mr Selvon carries, perhaps inevitably, a few chips on his shoulders.' Although the review speaks positively of Selvon's 'genuine talent', and recognises a 'Caribbean upsurge' of fiction writing, it lacks all conviction; when Richardson states that Selvon 'can give the impression of a character in the turn of a phrase', he is merely resorting to cliché. Given that Richardson knows nothing about Trinidad, his statement that Selvon 'handles the Trinidadian way of speech brilliantly' is self-consciously excessive in its praise, indicative (arguably) of the imperial habit of 'benevolence' to the native more than of critical integrity. In any case, the 'Trinidadian way of speech', having very low status as far as Richardson is concerned (we suspect), can have adjectives like 'brilliant', 'outstanding', 'excellent' or whatever heaped upon it, and yet remain a dunghill. True taste only emerges from an appreciation of the Queen's English, in the presence of which critics like Richardson are discerning in their use of adjectives.

The anonymous reviewer of Selvon's *Lonely Londoners* (1956) in the *Times* (6 December 1956) behaves differently from Richardson. Instead of gentlemanly condescension to the writing, there is cautious outrage at its political incorrectness. 'Mr Selvon is an intellectual born in Trinidad but of Indian parentage', the review begins, innocuously enough it seems. The following sentences however expose the reviewer's agenda: 'Nevertheless, he does not seem quite the right person to present the case for West Indian immigrants to Britain. Indeed, by presenting the average Caribbean as foul-mouthed, promiscuous and simple-minded, he does them some disservice.' Apart from responding simplistically to Selvon's characters, one's objection to the review is its presumption that Selvon's art should serve good race relations or some similar socio-political cause. In other words, because Selvon is 'Black', he should be community relations officer first, and artist second. The opening sentence is now capable of being distressed: Selvon is an 'intellectual', and as such should know better than to present the natives as 'natives'. He is, however, 'an intellectual born in Trinidad', so his shortcomings perhaps have to do with his colonial origin. If he is not quite an intellectual, neither is he quite a West Indian: he was 'born a Trinidadian *but* of Indian parentage.' Not

David Dabydeen

being quite an intellectual nor quite a West Indian mean that he is not 'quite the right person' to describe immigrant life in London. Needless to say, all of this would have come as a surprise to Selvon, who was totally Creolised, and who *never* thought of himself, nor wanted to be thought of, as an intellectual. Once again we may have here the case of White man describing the 'native' in ways unfamiliar to the 'native'; and the White man who determines which native is best qualified to speak on behalf of the natives.

The reviewer however is not a trenchant imperialist. Note the caution and hesitancy of his opening remarks, indicated by words like 'but', 'not quite' and 'nevertheless'. And even when he feels bold enough to press his charge, starting with the word 'indeed', he is not totally convinced of his correctness: hence he states that Selvon's portrayal of West Indians does them '*some* disservice'. Not *total* 'disservice', for perhaps the 'average Caribbean' *is* largely 'foul-mouthed, promiscuous and simple-minded'.

The reviewer suddenly changes tack by acknowledging in the following paragraph that '*The Lonely Londoners*, however, is primarily a poetic novel, not a social document,' but there is no commitment to making the case for Selvon's artistry. He pronounces on Selvon's 'effective' use of dialect, but even so, adds an immediate qualification: 'effective, if self-conscious, use of dialect'. Before getting totally mired in hesitancy, he then brings the review to a swift end.

Ifs and buts are not part of the vocabulary of Isabel Quigly, reviewer of Selvon's *An Island is a World* for the *Spectator* (15 April 1955). She is adamant about what she really really wants, and finds Selvon a limp and impotent disappointment. She regrets 'how closely the cast of an intelligent young West Indian's mind seems to resemble that of a young European; how, apart from the conscious passages of description and local colour, this novel might just as well have been written by an Englishman.' Isabel Quigly really really wants Selvon to be a Black caged and ferocious beast, but Selvon is a disappointing

King Kong. 'It is absurd to complain that Mr Selvon has got away, as undoubtedly he has, from his island; absurd to expect the vision of a primitive from one who is at least half sophisticated. But Mr Selvon at this stage has lost the directness of the one before acquiring the complexity of the other, a common occurrence in a world where the eye of innocence is given spectacles at the earliest age and in the remotest places.'

Such lament for lost primitivism recurs in many other reviews by different hands, in different guises. Words like 'primitive' (sometimes disguised as 'naturalistic'), 'charm' and 'childlike' are common, even as the reviewers take up politically correct positions against colonial exploitation. With the notable exception of Francis Wyndham, reviewers sought in West Indian fiction what was apparently absent in post-war Britain: colour, gaiety, innocence, virility. Such poignant desire for the characteristics of the Noble Savage ensured that West Indian writing was eagerly received by the literati, even as the real thing – the nigger – was being hunted down and hounded out of the neighbourhood.

Mulk Raj Anand

◆◆◆◆◆◆◆◆◆◆◆◆◆◆◆◆◆◆◆◆◆◆

A Writer in Exile

Mulk Raj Anand single-handedly forced Western opinion to take account of another India – not one of palaces, peacocks and maharajahs, but of the underclass: the coolies, untouchables, victims of oppressive caste.

Coming to London in the 1920s, he was a habitue of the Bloomsbury Set, and was valued by writers such as E. M. Forster. However the Bloomsbury aesthetic (which he later typified as 'the imperceptible stirrings of sensibilities of noble ladies') did not give him the form he needed for the social issues which became his chosen subject. Negotiating between 'the twin burden on my shoulders, the Alps of the European tradition and the Himalaya of my Indian past', he constructed his own prose style that drew on Indian storytelling tradition, incorporated Hindi and Punjabi words and attempted to communicate the distinctive quality of the speech of his Indian peasantry.

His contribution has been gargantuan, forming a bridge between the social novel of Dickens and Gissing and the home-grown deeply-felt issues of a country in the process of radical social and political change.

Going away from India to study philosophy was the first important departure point in my life. In his poem *Secrets of Self* Iqbal had suggested self-search as the key to becoming an integrated self. This search became inevitable for me when, in the autumn of 1925, I arrived in the UK to begin research for a doctorate in philosophy, working under the Kantian scholar Dawes Hicks. I was also to be advised by Bertrand Russell.

My mood at the time was existentialist, brought on by the agony of suffering as an innocent involved in the struggle for freedom in India. I had, after all, received seven stripes after the Jallianwala Bagh shooting in Amritsar. That incident coloured my approach to the Bloomsbury circle in London, which I entered through the courtesy of E. M. Forster and Leonard Woolf. No one in the Bloomsbury group mentioned anything about Indian freedom or even about British politics, but nevertheless at the regular Wednesday evening 'At Homes' I found myself reacting against the 'art for art's sake' attitudes of Clive Bell and Roger Fry. The talks I had with members of the group I recreated in my *Conversations in Bloomsbury*.

It was a vital difference with Edward Sackville-West which triggered my departure from Bloomsbury. He had asked, 'What are you writing?' I said, 'I have done a short novel about an outcaste . . .' 'Oh!', he replied, 'you can't do a novel about that kind of person! For example, one only laughs at cockneys, like Dickens does.' I realised later that the hostess of Bloomsbury, Virginia Woolf, was an upper-class patron who justified snobbery.

Leaving Bloomsbury, I went to Ireland to see my girlfriend Irene, about whom I write in my novel *The Bubble*. She was facing trial for alleged gun-running and was sent to jail for a year. I was deciding what to do next when I met the poet A. E. (George Russell), who was a theosophist. I told him what had happened in Bloomsbury. He said, 'Go to Gandhi for some time! He equates the struggle against untouchability with the struggle for Indian freedom.' A. E. wrote to Gandhi for me and then I wrote myself, asking to come to him.

Mahatma wrote back to me in January 1927, inviting me back to India. What happened when I saw Gandhi is recorded in my *Little Plays of Mahatma Gandhi*. I showed him a draft of my novel *Untouchable*, which I wrote at his retreat. 'Why such big words?' he asked. 'Untouchables sigh, moan, groan. They don't talk in big words.' I replied that I was following James Joyce, who coined words to create inner thoughts and emotions. Gandhi answered, 'Forget about Joyce. Write what people say.'

I re-wrote *Untouchable* in the light of Gandhi's *Talisman*, which prescribed that 'if you are in agony, go and help the man who may need help and your agony will disappear.' That perception of the human condition became the starting point of all my fiction writing. In *Untouchable* I wrote about a day in the life of my hero/anti-hero, Bakha. I took as my starting point my mother's insult to a real sweeper boy, Bakha, who had once brought me home hurt when I had been hit on the head by a stone thrown by a big boy in a fight while we were playing.

I gave the novel to the literary agent Curtis Brown to negotiate with a publisher. Nineteen of them turned it down. I realised that the human conditions of the disinherited were not considered proper for polite fiction in Britain. One publisher commented '*Untouchable* is untouchable!' I nearly committed suicide, but appreciation of the book by Naomi Mitchison, Storm Jameson, Edward Thompson and others gave me hope. After four years of anguish, Forster wrote a preface to it and a small firm, Wishart Booles, issued it. It received warm reviews.

In the meantime, on Gandhi's advice, I had gone round India, the south, east and centre, and seen the repression of the people by the imperial police, who resented the curfew imposed by the Viceroy during his regal tour from Delhi to Calcutta. Police oppression of the freedom fighters brought my protest against authority almost to the point of obsession. My pilgrimage across India also brought me into contact with all kinds of rejected human beings: landless labourers, women in villages going to fetch water from miles away, children in congested factories, beggars and destitutes. Several of these were to figure in my short stories.

Back in London in 1928, I continued my research for my doctor's degree. Through the critic Bonamy Dobrée I met T. S. Eliot. I worked for Eliot in the office of *The Criterion* and only stopped going to him when he declared that he was a royalist in politics, a classicist in literature and an Anglo-Catholic in religion. He was known to be editing Rudyard Kipling's verse and in one of our meetings he told me that he thought *Kim* was the greatest novel about India. I was outraged that a pseudo orphan Indo-Irish boy should be considered by the author of *The Wasteland* to be an ideal hero. In reaction I began to write a novel about a real orphan boy, Munoo, who was to be the hero/anti-hero of my next novel, *Coolie*. Unlike Kim, who serves a British intelligence officer and is a bit of a know-all, my orphan boy is uprooted from the soil, becomes the servant in a clerk's household, turns coolie, and ends his existence driving a mem-sahib in a rickshaw in Simla.

My second novel was received with great warmth and sold three impressions in a week. I had no difficulty with publishers or reviewers thereafter. Degradation of the expropriated peasant was my continuing theme in *Two Leaves and a Bud* and in *The Big Heart*. I was showing the division of the people into classes, on a tea plantation in Assam and in a craft community of coppersmiths when the machine was brought in, causing the unemployed workers to break it up as the machine wreckers had once done in Britain. I was affected by Ernst Toller's play, *The Machine Wreckers*, popular at this time, and I also read Karl Marx's *Letters on India*.

I realised in exile that, against the proud proclaimers of the powerful and their imposition of damnation, there *were* rebels, who insisted that man's evolution lies in his self-awareness, depth of feeling and emotional experience. One saw rescue from chaos through engagement with and commitment to life's processes.

With the publication of my first novels my interests extended from literature to the arts. I enjoyed the friendship not only of Bonamy Dobrée and Bertrand Russell, but also of Ludwig Wittgenstein, John Strachey, Aldous Huxley, Eric Gill, Herbert Read and Laurence Binyon. It was Read who encouraged me to write a little book called *Persian Painting*, which was published by the Criterion Miscellany Series at the time of the great exhibition of Persian art at the Royal Academy. It sold ten thousand copies and was followed by my *Hindu View of Art*.

Political work further widened my circle of acquaintances in London, particularly in the Labour movement. I belonged to the India League, which Bertrand Russell chaired, and I became friendly with Kingsley Martin, Harold Laski and Michael Foot. I returned to India every two years and so was able to keep in touch with Gandhi, Jawaharlal Nehru and Subhash Bose. I stayed at Santiniketan with the poet Rabindranath Tagore, whose benign influence opened me up to the humanist tradition of the Brahma Samaj, founded by Ram Mohan Roy. But it was back in Britain that I was politically active. After the Conference of World Writers against Fascism in 1936, over which Gorky presided, several of us formed the Progressive Writers Group in London. The emergence of Nazi fascism brought many younger British writers together in a common cause.

In various conferences of the awakened intelligentsia I represented India. Together we were able to create awareness of the freedom struggles in India, though as war approached I remained a conscientious objector because the Atlantic Charter, which Churchill and Roosevelt drafted, made no mention of India's freedom.

After the USSR was attacked by Hitler, I agreed to be a casual broadcaster in the India section of the BBC, working with George Orwell. We invited Chinese writers like Hsiao Chen and British authors such as Forster, Read and Eliot to become involved in a BBC magazine. Meanwhile I was influenced in what I call my 'anti-super attitudes' by my contemporaries, Ignazio Silone in Italy and André Malraux in France.

My exile in Europe helped me to understand larger literary connections and transitions. In the eighteenth-century novel, for example, I perceived three elements: the novelist himself, the characters he created, and the moral lesson. 'Dear Reader, you must not do what Moll Flanders did . . .' In nineteenth-century fiction there are only two elements: author and character, Thomas Hardy and Tess. There is no moral lesson about the landlord's son who rapes the heroine. Then comes James Joyce's *Ulysses*, where there is neither author nor 'Dear Reader', but only the feelings of Mr and Mrs Bloom in a stream of consciousness.

My novels gained from Joyce, but in my attendance at discussions in Virginia Woolf's circle I came to realise that the stream of consciousness method, when carried to the interior of a work – in *The Waves*, for example – ultimately led to the evaporation of the characters. I rejected Woolf's attack on Arnold Bennett and John Galsworthy because of their emphasis on characters.

I returned permanently to India in 1948. I had come to understand during my years in Britain that human destiny presents itself in political terms, whether one sides with those who pursue power and throw bombs on Hiroshima and Nagasaki to assist their imperial will, or is on the side of those who wish to connect in the world and reject the way in which it is torn up into power blocks, reducing the bulk of mankind to wretchedness beyond wretchedness. I have been writing in a time of change. My characters, with their subjective feelings, emerge from the vague interiors of past fiction to face the facts of human life in all their contradictions. This emphasis was born of my exile in Britain.

Dom Moraes

❖❖❖❖❖❖❖❖❖❖❖❖❖❖❖❖❖❖

Changes of Scenery

Dom Moraes has, at his very best, a felicity of language that speaks clearly of his root vocation of lyric poetry.

The conditions of his early life sharpened his poetic sensibility. The only child of one of India's journalistic lions, Frank Moraes, Dom Moraes had had a peripatetic and intense childhood, but a home in which the great and the good – from East and West – were familiar guests. Poetry was an early discovery. At fifteen, he had already been praised by W. H. Auden and published by Stephen Spender. (The latter met him when he came to Bombay on a visit, and told him something that Moraes says wryly he has never forgotten: 'Writing poetry is like looking into a succession of mirrors, and as you write more and more of it, the face you see in the mirror becomes more and more horrible.')

London literati however saw only grace and immense sensitivity, an accomplished aesthetic, and the rarity value of an Indian writer choosing not the novel form but poetry. Awarded the prestigious Hawthornden Prize in 1958, he also confounded expectations by writing as responsively to Wordsworth's 'bony sorrow' as to 'the hot verandahs where the chauffeurs drowse' of his childhood home. Suspended, in a sense, between worlds, he raises questions as to whether his poetry is the by-product of his chosen location, or the consolation of it.

I arrived in England in August 1954. The P & O liner *Strathmore* decanted me at Tilbury. I was 16 years old. My possessions were a suitcase full of clothes and a steamer trunk full of books.

I also carried a small portable typewriter, only slightly younger than I was. My father had used it in Burma and China, where he had been a war correspondent. The London editor of his newspaper, the *Times of India*, an amiable man named Mulgaonkar, met me off the ship, and escorted me on the train trip to London. Showers had fallen as the *Strathmore* docked, but the clouds had moved away and from the train window the landscape, rinsed by rain, looked newly washed. Though I had never seen it before, I recognised it from books.

There were occasional glimpses of very green countryside. Mostly there were endless, uniform rows of redbrick houses that faced away from me; clothes hung up to dry in their backyards, given shapes by the wind. They faced other, identical houses. Pink-skinned people went in and out of the houses; typewriter ribbons of road unwound between them. The traffic was slow and intermittent; it was still early in the day. I identified shops that were not yet open, and an undertaker's establishment that was. Near London I began to see Black people, shabbily dressed, and groups of long-haired youths in Edwardian clothes. I recognised them as Jamaican immigrants and Teddy boys, from novels read under the humid sun of Bombay.

London seemed familiar too, when we reached it. It was then still identifiable as an English city. Its great grey buildings aroused a sense of history in me. I knew the streets by name. Somewhere in the labyrinth they formed, a key to my future lay. Somewhere in it there were poets I had read. Soon I might meet them. I certainly knew I would meet Stephen Spender, who had read my poems in India and had published some of them in *Encounter*. So, though I had never been to England before, it did not seem to me a strange or an unknown country. It seemed to me the destination I had been trying to reach for years, a hidden place inside myself, to arrive in which was a relief and a sudden freedom.

Through Mulgaonkar I found a small flat in Knightsbridge. It was really a bedsitter, but had an attached bathroom, an electric kettle and a minuscule electric stove. I lived in it for

several months. I had two years to wait before my Oxford
college would admit me. Though I was too young for university,
it was in this flat, in a small way, that I started my literary
career. I did it all the wrong way round. A young English writer
would have entered university and met other writers there.
Then for a couple of years he might have been led by what used
to be called a bohemian life. Finally he would have found his
way into the literary establishment, and rubbed shoulders with
the great men and women authors of his time.

Thanks to Stephen Spender and his wife Natasha, the last bit
came first where I was concerned. The Spenders were very
caring people; they felt I would be lonely in London. They
invited me to lunch every Sunday at their house in St John's
Wood. These Sunday lunches were attended by other guests,
usually famous writers. The first one was Cyril Connolly, who
told me my suit didn't fit and reduced me to tremulous silence.
I was nearly always silent, unable to think of anything to say. I
listened to the conversation around me, however, and came to
the conclusion that great writers were no less silly than other
human beings, and quite often much sillier. It was a valuable
discovery for a young man to make.

Stephen also introduced me to older writers like E. M. Forster
and Walter de la Mare. So my poems were read and criticised
by several people whose work had formed part of my mind. I
sometimes could not believe my good luck, and was grateful
for it. Stephen then tried to introduce me to writers nearer my
own age. During the week he occasionally asked me to lunch
near the *Encounter* offices in Haymarket. The others present
were young poets whose work he liked. One, Oliver Bernard,
took me into Soho, in whose cagelike pubs and drinking clubs
a wide selection of artistic fauna was to be found. I met some
good writers and painters there, and found friends in Francis
Bacon and George Barker. I also encountered David Archer.

Why nobody has ever written a biography of David is beyond
me. He was a great man. He was tall and, when I met him,
fiftyish and rather bald, with the flushed face of a drinker, and

very kind, bespectacled eyes of that pale blue colour which physiognomists have described as a mark of criminal tendencies. Archer walked with an awkward tensity of body, a Prussian stiffness, a bundle of newspapers always clamped under his left arm. He looked as though he were afraid he would explode. He had a rich father, whose fortune he had slowly demolished through his patronage of the arts. Whenever David had money, he gave it away, almost at random, but mostly to needy writers and to the sailors he liked to sleep with.

He had started a literary bookshop in the 1930s. This was in Parton Street, a cul-de-sac off Red Lion Square. From this shop, under the imprint of The Parton Press, he published three of the most important books of poetry of the decade. These were the first books of George Barker, Dylan Thomas, and David Gascoyne. During the war the shop and David moved to Glasgow. Here the Parton Press produced W. S. Graham's first book. The war ended; David came back to London and opened the third Parton Bookshop in Greek Street, Soho. It was a beautiful establishment on two floors; besides the section which sold new books, it contained a library, a coffee shop, and an art gallery where homeless poets sometimes slept.

This bookshop became bankrupt very soon, due to its proprietor's habit of never accepting any money from his customers. Indeed he often gave them whatever was in the till, feeling they looked in need of a square meal. Before this happened, he offered to publish my first book of poems. I protested that he had not read any. 'But, my dear boy, I only ever read detective stories,' he said. 'I never read any of the poets I published. But I can smell a poet, if you see what I mean.' He then seemed to realise the possible implications of his remark. 'I don't mean that none of you ever bathe,' he added hastily, 'except Dylan, you could certainly smell him, what?' For some reason he always talked like a Wodehouse character.

But in July 1957 he published my first book, *A Beginning*. We had to distribute it by carrying it round the bookshops, some of whom grudgingly accepted a few copies on sale or return.

But suddenly and unexpectedly it started to get good reviews everywhere, from rather well-known poets. The bookshops started to order copies. Then it won the Hawthornden Prize.

My father was educated at Oxford. Afterwards he entered Lincoln's Inn and emerged from it a qualified barrister. He returned to Bombay, where his legal career proved brief and unsatisfactory. He joined the *Times of India*, which was owned by a British company and where most of his colleagues on the editorial staff were English. In 1937 he married his college sweetheart. A year later I was born. With all his British connections, it was rather surprising that he was a strong supporter of the Indian Freedom Movement. Jawaharlal Nehru was a friend of his. When the government cracked down on the Congress party, my parents hid several leaders, wanted by the police, in our flat, where they shared my nursery.

If his British employers knew about this, they did not let it affect them. As a journalist my father was brilliant. They made him the first Indian war correspondent, and he was despatched to the Burma front, and later to China. During his absence, a lengthy one, my mother, who was gifted and pretty and a practising pathologist, went quietly mad. My father returned. In 1946 he accepted the editorship of the *Times of Ceylon*, and we spent the next two years in Colombo. Then he went back to Bombay and his old paper, which in 1949 sent him on an assignment to Australia and New Zealand. From Australia the Indian prime minister, Nehru, asked him to travel through southeast Asia and report on the state of the nations there.

My father, because he was very worried about my mother's mental health, had taken us both with him. When we had got back to India, she had a complete breakdown, became violent, and had to be committed to a mental hospital. She had still been in it when I left for England. It was possibly this that forced my father to send me there two years before I could be admitted to Oxford. There was nobody at home to look after me. Also, I continually told him how much I hated India and actually feared it. I had the same feelings about it as I did about my mother. I felt she had betrayed me and that I had no home. There were other reasons. I had never learnt, and I could not speak, any of the Indian languages, only English.

At this time, very shortly after Independence, there was a kind of chauvinism in Indian attitudes. It was felt that an adolescent of Indian birth in a newly independent India *had* to speak an Indian language, *had* to feel Indian. I rebelled against this assumption, but was constantly reminded of it by my schoolmates and the adults I met. Since my childhood I had spent much of my time reading, and the language I read was English. That was also the language I wrote in, and writing in it was the most important part of my life. Sometimes in Bombay I was told that I should not even speak it, or not exclusively; it was unpatriotic. My inclinations, even then, were to do the opposite of what others told me I should do.

My father knew all the powerful people in his country. Because he was now the editor of the largest and most influential English language newspaper, he was one of them. They talked to him as an equal, and often took his advice, and to them it did not seem to matter that he could only speak to them in English. He felt, however Westernised he was, that he was Indian. He felt that he belonged to India. He did not understand my reaction to the country of both our births, but he knew it existed. He also, I think, realised that he could not change it. That was why he surrendered and why he sent me to England two years before it was necessary. However reluctantly, however sadly, he realised that in India I felt an outsider.

In England I never felt an outsider. I lived in London for a year and made several friends, not all of them literary. Then for a year I travelled in Europe, and stayed for long periods in Paris and Rome. When I returned to London I felt I had come home. In October 1956 I had to make another adjustment; I went up to Jesus College, Oxford. At that time most young men did National Service before university, and at 18 I was the youngest person in my college. But I was more grown up than most of the other undergraduates. I had travelled more widely than anyone else in college, I had published poetry in several reputable literary magazines, and, important in a society of young males, I had experience with women.

A Beginning was published and reviewed in my first year; it won the Hawthornden Prize in my second. I was not yet twenty. I was the youngest person ever to win the award, and the first non-English writer. The results were a cyclone of publicity, which was bad for me. What was good was that I received offers from national magazines and newspapers to review books and write feature articles. I began to know a lot of people, none of whom except for Mulgaonkar, were Indians, until Ved Mehta arrived in Oxford. He was blind, and had written an autobiographical book. He became my friend not because he was an Indian, but because he was a writer. Nearly all his other friends were Indians, though they were not writers.

They were his friends because they were Indians. They found comfort and reminders of home in one another's company. I needed no such reassurances. It didn't matter to me where my friends came from, nor even, any longer, where I came from. The language I wrote was the language spoken and understood by everyone around me. I fitted into English life, but the concept of 'home' was difficult for me to hold on to. One lived where one was; different places were only changes of scenery. Once I had left Oxford, publishers and television companies hired me to write books and documentary scripts. Magazines and newspapers paid me to travel. Sometimes I was sent to India, and I found I did not have any quarrel with it now.

During this time I had a number of adventures with women; then I married. Judy was English. She could hardly have been more English. She came of a county family, generations of which had lived in Buckinghamshire. Her father was dead, but her mother was still young. At weekends we visited her in the country. We bought a house in Islington. We had a son. Judy was a very good person, but I was hardly an ideal husband. I travelled too much, sometimes into dangerous situations like

Dom

wars; I drank too much. After six years, we decided to separate. Soon after this I was offered the editorship of a magazine in Hong Kong. The position involved constant travel in southeast Asia and Australia. I took it.

Three years later the United Nations hired me as a literary adviser. I was based in New York, but travelled incessantly, and produced two books. My UN agency then lent me to the Government of India to write television films. I did not now dislike India, but the work bored me, and I resigned and wrote a biography of Mrs Indira Gandhi, whom I knew well, and also a book on Bombay. Judy and I remained friends. Whenever I visited London I saw her, and our son Heff. During one of these visits from India, it occurred to me that England was the country I knew best, and I was tired of travel. I had lunch with my literary agent, who was also a friend, and announced my intention of returning to England and setting up shop there.

I had expected him to be delighted. He was appalled. 'Don't you realise,' he said, 'that you've been away ten years? It's a hell of a long time. The editors and television producers have all changed; even the publishers are different now. You'd have to start from scratch. If I were you, I would go back to India, make it your base, and write about Asia.' This conversation had a shattering effect on me. It was not easy to accept the role of a man everybody had forgotten. I talked to other close friends and, usually with reluctance, they gave me the same advice as my agent. So I flew back to India. Changes of scenery had become part of my life. I might as well be a part of the Indian scenery as that of another place.

Last time I went back to London it was winter. That was three years ago. I had flown in from Israel. In Jerusalem I had met one of the closest friends I have ever had, the poet T. Carmi. I had said goodbye to him for the last time; he was dying of cancer. Judy had died two years earlier also of cancer; she had been tragically young. But Heff still lived in London, where he was a successful music mixer. He owned a house in Islington, not the same one Judy and I had had, and I stayed with him there. He developed a bad cold and had to stay in bed much of the time. One day, feeling very fatherly, I decided to make him some soup. I put it on to cook and looked out of the window at the English winter.

It was evening; I saw uniform redbrick houses, rooftops and television aerials under the dull, stationary clouds. It was by no means a romantic or beautiful view, but to me tremendously evocative. The familiar smell of London came in through the window, and mingled with the smell of chicken soup. I had first come here as a refugee, fleeing from his birthplace to another country of which he had had great expectations. England had fulfilled most of my expectations, but I no longer belonged here or anywhere. This, to me, seemed an important piece of knowledge, which it had taken over half a century to acquire. In London I had visited the pubs and restaurants I had once frequented, at least those that remained, and had talked to old friends.

I had done what I had come for. Next day I was to fly back to India. There I had poems to finish, and a woman whom I loved to meet. I took the soup in to Heff, who sat up and blew his nose. We talked about my departure while he consumed the soup. 'You seem very happy today,' he said. 'Is it because you're in London, or because tomorrow you're going back to India?' It was a very good question. I looked at him, thought of several matters I had never told him of, and offered the only possible reply. 'Honestly,' I said, 'I don't know.'

Buchi Emecheta

••••••••••••••••••••••••

Crossing Boundaries

Buchi Emecheta shot to prominence in the 1970s with a series of novels depicting the struggles of a Nigerian-born single mother in London. Hugely successful, these novels were unique in their exploration of the post-Second World War settlers from West Africa who are often overlooked in Britain. Since then she has combined her fiction writing with work as an academic, lecturing in the United States, Nigeria and Britain.

I have been in this profession of storytelling for almost three decades. I am still not sure if I am regarded as a literary artist, an academic or a mere novelist. Theorists have found it difficult to wrap and parcel me in a neat compartment. Preferably with a tidy label.

Quite recently I gave my latest work to a Western publisher friend to read for an opinion before embarking on rewriting. 'The gist is that it is a lovely and moving story about.... But it is very difficult to place. Most Western publishers would not know into which category to slot it. It is not a thriller, but I find it hard to put down once I have got into it. And it is not a commercial blockbuster. The suspense kept me on and I am still thinking about the subject.'

I thanked this highly placed publisher. Then I asked myself, 'Why should I be a category? What is so bad in recounting our experiences, cultures, dreams and visions in our own anecdotal fashion? Is it because that genre is not Western? But it is African, Caribbean and Asian. Surely if the true voice of an artist is to be heard it must be permitted to emit from the inner tremblings of the artist's emotional culture. In the genre he is accustomed to. True in the cultural passage, I am fast losing my emotional language, but still not the art of recounting my story.

I was raised in a culture where face to face communication is vital. In my early school days, the best day of the week was Friday. On this day, we brought our own brooms, sponges and soap to wash and clean out our classrooms. Then we had a lunch break during which time the Head went round and awarded marks for the cleanest class. After the break it was storytelling time. The class with the lowest mark would be excluded from story time. The proud teacher of the cleanest class would call out, 'Story time'. And we the children would shout back, 'Entertainment!' And at the same time call out the names of favourite storytellers.

A little girl would stand up and tell the story of the tortoise who went to steal yams not knowing that the farmer had stuck magic glue all around his farm. And the tortoise was stuck until the farmer came the following day. The best part was when the little girl started to dance and sing the tortoise's song of apology. The girl would demonstrate the way tortoise danced with his house on his back, or the way he tried to unglue himself from the magical glue. And the whole class did the same behind our desks, answering to the call song of the storyteller. And when we had had enough of one storyteller, another would be nominated. Looking back now, I recall that most of those youngsters were not particularly what we now call academic, but they became quite well known in our school community. And there is no doubt that the confidence they gained that early in life is helping them still.

On Fridays, at the end of the school week, we went home with story songs in our hearts ready for the weekend.

Sundays were Bible stories. Listen to an African churchman preaching. He takes just one line from the Bible and weaves it into the stories of his ancestors, channelling it through his hopes and dreams. At the end of it all is a moral twist.

In Lagos there were the singing beggars, and the street story-tellers in music. Children trailed behind them listening and sometimes taking part in their dances. I personally liked following twin mothers whenever they came to our street to sing and proclaim their happiness at being the mother of twins.

At home in the evenings, some aunts and houseboys told stories in front of the house for all the tenants' children until we fell asleep.

There were radios, but these were for adults. My father's generation went to an open field called Rowe Park. There a pale, curiously shaped box hung on a tree. The workers stood under the tree in the evenings, listening to the news and returned to their families, noisy and argumentative, talking about something they called Independence. When most people became rich enough to buy their own radios, women noticed that their menfolk missed the face to face arguments and opinions.

I was even more sensitised to the art of listening and story-telling by the big mothers in the village. Whenever we went to the village, we had to listen to the old ladies. Their stories were particularly poignant because theirs were told in Igbo language, and by women who had never been to big cities like Lagos.

When father passed on, and I moved to my maternal uncle in Pike Street, his son who had been to the UK bought our very own radio – then called Rediffusion. On Saturday evenings, this Yoruba woman called Ome Boku commanded our attention. She did not see her listeners, because she told her stories over the wireless. But she brought the face to face feeling in her voice. She introduced herself fully, giving her full praise names. This was followed by a long greeting and prayers to all her listeners and she would hope that her story made us wiser and thoughtful. She burst into songs between the stories. She ended by praising herself again and prayed for all of us. This became the height of family gathering at the weekends. But like most things Nigerian, she was soon pushed out of the slot. It was claimed that her stories were not so innocent because she was using them to uncover some uncomfortable political truths.

Omo Boku did talk about animals, and a great deal about the little happenings of everyday life. Yet she made the rulers uncomfortable. I missed her.

I missed her a lot because, soon after, I moved into a boarding school, which was very Western, very Christian and very modern. And such indulgences like storytelling were regarded as gossip if not complete paganism.

The day I stepped into Methodist Girls High school, I was uprooted from my culture, and I made my first great step into the Western world. Most of us new girls did not understand what our teachers were saying, since they came from high institutions like Oxford and Cambridge. The only way we could communicate was between ourselves when our teachers were out of earshot. If you were caught speaking in vernacular you paid a penny fine.

One young English teacher from the Midlands said to us innocently, 'I always know when you are speaking Yoruba, because your voices were raised, you all would be rather noisy and full of laughter.' That should have taught anyone that our being forced to pay fines for speaking our mother tongue was like cutting our tongues of joy from our heads. But at the time, we were being made to feel privileged for attending such a school and being taught by Europeans.

It took years of suppressing one's mother tongue to be able to think and communicate in English. But you cannot eradicate your past, not completely. Yet, I am being told indirectly, 'I wish you'd stop being an African storyteller.'

Though as our people say, a child that stayed too long in the market is lost to its parents. After a stay of over thirty years one had stayed over too long. Consequently I am neither English nor fully African, but part of a group of floating people I refer to in my recent book as the new tribe. If I had been White I would have no problem. But I noticed that my listeners in places like Milan, Munich and even among the Mothers' Union in my local church, cannot understand why a greater part of me still clings to Africa. They overlook the fact that my colour will always be my badge.

And this Black badge coupled with the hybrid of upbringing leads to the kind of isolation that is almost eternal. You cannot confide to your friend and age-mate in London about the difficulties you are going through in your work. She probably is a cleaner or at best a nurse who is coping with survival and to her, reading books is something for other people. In Africa, women relatives regard you as a money bag. They confuse popularity with wealth, and you are labelled as stingy. Among the few White people who summon up the courage to acknowledge your 'Good morning', you are always a Black woman aiming above her position. If on the other hand, I were of mixed race, with a milky chocolate colour, my burden of isolation would be comparatively lighter. But I am not. And since I am endowed with the rich skin tone of my forebears, and their cultural gift of recounting the past in words and music, I do not feel too alone in my middle-class abode in London suburbia.

Isolation can be turned into gold. I am not one of the greats in my profession, but I am one of the most persistent, one of the most tenacious, and one of the most outspoken. My song is sung mostly through the voices of Black women characters I create from looking around me. Women who lived during the time of my mother, women who raised their families alone when their husbands were fighting the wars for White people, women who for economic reasons find themselves in White Western cities doing the jobs nobody wanted, women who endured the brutality of disappointed men, and women whose voices had been silenced through ignorance.

Isolation in England gave me the kind of freedom to talk about discrimination women faced and are still facing in education. Subtle gender harassment through ridicule. And for the few women who had made it and whose voices are being heard, the burden of responsibilities tied to their backs conjures the picture of overladen camels forced to run up a steep hill.

I am not the only Black woman singing this song. There are quite a number of us, but our works are mainly relegated to the margins. But we soldier on.

For an African woman to make the best of isolation, she must have gone through a baptism of fire. But here I am grateful to my early English educators.

I got a scholarship to a very, very middle-class school. I was among girls from rich homes and I was the only Igbo girl among two hundred Yorubas. This was like being the only Black girl in an all-White elitist school. Mine was made worse because I came from a poor family and my mother never visited me because she thought I was wasting my life in not getting married that early. The family needed the money from my bride-price to educate my brother. So I seldom went home on holidays. These days when I watch the life of street children, I am reminded of what it was like. The pain and humiliation to a sensitive child is crushing. I still have never gone in depth about that part of my life, but suffice to say I survived by learning to get inner sustenance from inside my spiritual self. So isolation to me in later life was no longer strange.

I can read, I can read and I can read. And I can imagine. Now crowds can sometimes be intimidating. But I know of the well-being of my immediate family, living, as they say in the West, at the end of the telephone.

Would I have written my books if I had stayed in Nigeria? I doubt it. I doubt it very much. My husband burned my first manuscript. He said much later he did it to save me from myself. God rest his soul. Much harm is done by people who mean well. In Nigeria, the society, our society, would understand why he burned it. Sadly, I still don't. So I packed myself and my children and left. I wrote about it, and the experience formed my first autobiographical novels. I could not have done all that in Nigeria. My children would have been taken away from me, first by my people who would ask him to raise them, and then by my husband's family who would claim they have the right to them. And all they would have done would have been to use them as house servants in their own homes. I went through that and I swore my children would never live like that.

So all I had to worry about in England at the time was relative poverty. Because my children were never hungry thanks to rice, peas and meat (when meat was said to be good for children) and free school dinners. We did not get family support or family income supplement or one-parent family income. Maybe that was why I worked so hard and wrote so many books in such a short time. The children helped. They did paper rounds when they were old enough. Maybe that is why none of them ever thought of going on Social Security. They would rather work, however lowly.

If I had lived in Nigeria, my writing or storytelling or song would have taken another form. A much more acceptable female form. I would be permitted to tell my woes in the moonlight in a remote village, lamenting and dreaming about what might have been.

But I can no longer do that. I have acquired such a rich and cultural baggage – a village child, a city person, a single mother, a widow, a Christian, a traditionalist.

Yet I do miss the village background. I sometimes miss the markets, the smell of peppers, garri and ogiri, the vibrant churches, the over-dressing and life where every day is a celebration.

To have things both ways is impossible. So I live in compromise. I visit Africa often. I have a home there and my writings have aspects of both worlds. I tell the world about my Africa, usually the Africa of my dreams. And I describe my world market wandering to the people of my Africa. A tall order. But as my listeners in Brixton Library said to me recently, my type of writing does not belong to a neat package.

What they were saying is this: writers like us are too large for neat containers.

Rukhsana Ahmad

◆◆◆◆◆◆◆◆◆◆◆◆◆◆◆◆◆◆◆◆◆◆◆

In Search of a Talisman

Rukhsana Ahmad is a quiet, determined, principled explorer.
Seeking to construct her own set of goals, values and loyalties,
she has worked across a wide front – written plays (for stage and
radio), translated and edited verse, and written fiction.

Her robust intelligence, directed by a keen sense of academic
discipline, means that she takes pains with which genre she uses.
The Hope Chest, her first novel, focuses on the cultural constraints
on women – a subject very close to her heart – and dissects the
traumas undergone by three very different women – two in
Pakistan (the privileged daughter of the house and the far-from-
privileged daughter of a servant of the house) and one in London.
It was noteworthy for (amongst other elements) the compassionate
portrait of the snobbish, infuriating, convention-driven mother of
a rebellious Pakistani daughter, proving that Ahmad's fight for
justice for women is perceptive as well as persistent.

Memory is like a prism. Far too willing to deflect the past
into what you want to make of it. Given the Sisyphean
task of survival in a world we did not choose and cannot control
– few of us could manage without some genius for selective
recall. Call it a talent or a frailty, it is a tendency that makes
most autobiographical accounts deeply suspect. Except for
certain kinds of political writing I remain largely sceptical of the
genre and its validity as a historical document, whether at a

personal or sociological level. Certainly, it cannot be taken at face value.

Why, then, would I choose to embark upon this course myself? I could argue that writing is my version of political activism, that my own history as a writer has a strong political dimension, which grew and unfolded as I battled with the angel that has never quite stopped haunting my table. Pretend that mine is a story relevant to all women. Insist that I will not rationalise blunders, or omit details to camouflage motives. Use every ploy to project *my* reality in defence of my choices. For how else would you absolve yourself of the usual plethora of follies and aberrations that typify human experience? Or survive the pain of remembering the past in its entirety? Surely these are all legitimate stratagems for the diarist – and using them would be a pardonable offence.

But instead I decided to shed those pretences and admit certain biases in the hope that charting the journey from Karachi to London, which wrought a sea-change both in my life and my work, might reveal some hidden truth about myself as a writer; a secret catch that would release me from the need to construct barriers to my own progress, which I consistently do, to this day. But perhaps this too is just another caveat offered in the spirit in which manufacturers place health warnings on packets of cigarettes, reasonably certain that they will not actually deter the real addicts.

The conjunction between my development as a writer and my life here is especially difficult for me to unravel because I live in a state of chronic amnesia, imposed, at least in part, by a dogged optimism. After the briefest mourning I tend to put failures and mistakes behind me, labelling them as prerequisites to learning and progress, along a lesser-known route to glory which the future (filled with promise!) will bring to light very soon. In fact, this determination to proclaim the triumph of hope over experience has made the past a dangerous place for me to visit. Remembering is fraught with danger. Suddenly, it dredges up ghosts weighted down and buried in haste after a fierce battle. Yet, in these pages, once again, I risk the gloom where the might-have-beens of my life lurk, hoping *this* expedition will bring forth a talisman instead of disturbing them! Hoping they will lie still.

A stratagem I learnt early in my life was to hoard every emblem of success and destroy all evidence of failure. Every certificate of merit, every prize, every commendation and every piece of writing of which I felt proud I kept in a drawer in my mother's house. All of these – my most cherished belongings – I left behind, in the care of my sister when I got married and came to London for the first time. I would take them with me only once I felt certain of my future. They stayed there until after I had my first baby, almost three years later.

I was marrying a man of whom I knew very little – but I had tremendous clarity about why I was marrying at all. It was to escape the powerlessness of the state of girlhood in which I could, in theory, be trapped till the end of my days, in the bosom of a deeply traditional family which expected me to live by the rules that were applied from the time I had entered puberty. Dusk was our official curfew.

Ours was a fairly orthodox middle-class (though often financially hard pressed) home. Its very walls were seeped in the bitterness of a deeply unhappy marriage – out of which my mother had not been able to find an escape route except that of resignation and prayers. Although to this day she has neither lost her faith in the absolute necessity for marriage nor her reflexive anxiety for any young woman who has crossed twenty-four without a serious prospect in sight, as far back as I can remember, she had a serious commitment to the 'empowerment' (my word) of women through education and a career. *She* saw these, however, as necessary 'preparation' for unforeseen misfortune: death or divorce, or an unexpected financial disaster, never as an alternative to marriage. (In Pakistan, to this day, few women escape marriage and very few choose divorce. They rarely live alone as unmarried women.)

My father was a construction engineer who had qualified

from a provincial college, not a proper university. He remembered with some awe the fateful moment when he'd been lucky enough to be recruited as an officer, having been hand picked 'quite randomly by a real British army officer, out of a huge crowd of applicants'. He always boasted of being 'a self-made man', glad of the increase in income, the power and material comforts that officer status had brought him. Both my parents had lived through very harsh and hungry years raised by their widowed mothers in a world where the concept of a 'social services safety net' did not exist and the phrase 'single parent' had never been heard of. They used those childhood memories to instil the fear of failure into all of us – we were all expected to work hard. University education was the precious gift they never had. Success at school was instantly rewarded and applauded for days.

In a very large family you learn to share things and spaces and you also come to grips with competition: in its cruellest sense of competition for resources. Needless to say, at that level, a brand new unmarked book was a rare treat, much more so than new clothes. We all had those for the Muslim festival of Eid every now and then. My father had thirteen children, from three wives, and though we did not all live under the same roof, we were all dependent on one man's income for a fairly large chunk of my childhood years. 'There must be more money . . .!' was not a mere whisper that rustled politely through the house; it was almost a scream! Our worst years were peppered with the very real misery of violence and abuse when that scream turned into a row. My father had the most fearful temper that shot up in seconds. Family meals, a compulsory ritual, were not entirely free of hazard. At a fairly young age I learnt to sniff out danger and step into choppy conversations to skilfully avert disaster.

Quite early in life I discovered that my mother had shed a few tears at my birth – I was the third consecutive daughter she had borne. Sadly, I must concede, that it was an understandable response in that milieu. However, if aunts or uncles repeated that story before me my parents hastened to comfort me with their claim that I was the Lakshmi of the family who had brought good luck and the baby brother who followed me. (My father's career had leapt ahead the year I was born and he never begrudged me some credit for that and I gratefully accepted the credit for being the portent for my brother's birth.) However, my knowledge of her tears remained to underline the obvious differential in the status of male and female offspring within our household, within the extended family and within the community at large. Years later, when I discovered and translated Ishrat Aafreen's poetry, I found a few lines that put a social context on my mother's sorrow which finally erased my residual guilt for having caused them.

I understand better now why *Dombey and Son* should have moved me to such deeply felt empathy for poor Florence! Or, why Ismat Chughtai's *Crooked Line*, which captures the rough and tumble and the vague sense of neglect at the heart of that experience, should have been such a compelling read. Beyond that, of course, were the compensations of growing up in a large but close-knit family. I must admit we had plenty of fun together growing up in those less dangerous times, with considerably more freedom as children than middle-class parents would dare to risk in present day Karachi. Entire teams for card games, board games, ball games, cricket or hockey could be whistled up at the drop of a hat.

The year which would have been my happiest in that home ended in tragedy when my brother, a young airforce pilot at twenty, was killed in a hijacking incident. An incredible horror – barely mitigated by the gallantry award and hero's status he had earned by staking his own life. It was small comfort that he believed in what he *chose* to do. We were all shattered, but none so irreparably as my mother was. The house turned into a mausoleum. Many more young men died later that year. His loss remained – to confirm my rejection of patriotism and war over which we had argued often during his brief career. He in defence of it, my sister and I in vocal opposition to a culture that promotes them too vigorously.

The 'wars' that I have since observed in Britain have deeply underscored that conviction. When those reports on the Falklands adventure came, and, later, much more comprehensive television coverage of the Gulf War flashed endlessly on our screens, the one reality that was painfully clear to me was that young men were dying on both sides – and each death would permanently scar several lives. I went to Hyde Park religiously on Saturdays to attend the peace rallies – pained by my first insight into how marginal liberal British opinion really was! The marches were little more than an escape valve for an establishment broadly supported in its basest enterprises by the mainstream.

Anyhow, I felt much better for being able to protest. The ability to take direct action has been England's greatest gift to me. The very first rally I ever attended was a CND march. I had converted to Socialism in my Karachi University days, but I had never believed I could change or influence the system in any way – except through my writing. That I knew would ultimately be my chosen sphere of action.

Amongst the memorabilia I had left behind were the Departmental magazine I had edited as a student of English literature, a couple of short stories and a half-hearted translation of Manto, begun at the instigation of one of my tutors – who did not decry Urdu literature. A rare exception! The rest of the Department saw England, more precisely Oxbridge, as the seat of all learning, and English Literature as the crown of all knowledge. Some of them admitted concessions to Tolstoy and Dostoevsky; the Head, a deeply traditional Bengali, adored W. B. Yeats but also rated Nazrul Islam, Tagore and Iqbal – in what order, I cannot now remember.

It must have been in those days that I destroyed the 'manuscript' of the very first novel I had ever attempted. All twenty-six pages of it – my first serious attempt at writing – begun when I was a little under twelve. For someone who had been sent, at great personal cost to my parents, exclusively to English medium schools, it was a display of considerable stamina and a kind of failure: the manuscript was in Urdu. Clearly, at that stage I must have believed it was easier to take on the stylistic challenges of Urdu, although teaching of Urdu at the convent was quite minimal. It was taught only as a second language. Coached by an uncle, who was a schoolteacher, and influenced by our cousins who lived upstairs and attended the P. E. C. H. S. Government School round the corner from us, where the blue and white billboard at the gate declared its status in parenthesis (Urdu medium) beneath its name, my sisters and I had graduated to an advanced reading age in Urdu remarkably early, by convent standards.

I can still see the title of my first literary attempt, *Zard Patta* (*The Yellow Leaf*) as I had calligraphed it, painstakingly with thick flourishes and feathery tails on dog-eared foolscap lined paper. Secretly, I had hoped, it would be found, like the early attempts of the Brontës, to be admired by posterity after my tragically premature demise. For who else but a dead bore would want to cross thirty? Pity some of that carefree disdain for life does not stretch into one's middle age when the reality of death stalks so much closer!

Fortunately, in my heart of hearts, I knew better, and the text did not survive. I remember my heroine well: pale, tremulous, forever tearful! There were purple passages filled with clichés and pages galore about Nature in sympathetic mourning, designed to bring tears to the reader's eyes.

Without a doubt that poor heroine owed much of her characterisation to the soggiest Urdu romances which we devoured in secret, together with the slim weekly issues of Ibn-e-Safi's detective fiction (Urdu's answer to Sherlock Holmes) indiscriminately lumbered together with Dickens, Jane Austen and Mark Twain. The latter were, of course, permitted reading. Then there was the contraband literature which constituted research. Ours was not a liberal culture: even Manto and Chughtai were frowned upon as 'unsuitable' for children. Without second-hand copies of Ian

Fleming, Henry Miller, Lawrence, and all those innumerable *True Life* and *True Romance* which we kept hidden, wedged between the wardrobe and the dressing room wall, we would have remained woefully ignorant on that perennially taboo subject: SEX! In the absence of television, games and reading were our main entertainment.

During my undergraduate years I came to realise that the English Department of Karachi University definitely sneered at Urdu literature for its embarrassing sentimentality and 'lack of sophistication'. The staff had little contact with the Urdu Department which began half way down the corridor on the same floor. Although considerable lip service was paid to Urdu as the national language, in the real world of jobs and employment opportunities, Urdu-medium people had a lesser value than the English-medium inheritors of the Queen's language. Urdu was only marginally better off than the regional languages. The country is still ruled by people who are heirs to a ruling Western élite.

How could I have stood by the false start of many years ago? I never attempted writing in Urdu again, even after my graduation. Not that I couldn't any more; though I had lost some of my fluency and ease with it, I do believe I still could have managed to write reasonably well in Urdu if my education had not firmly persuaded me that literature was the preserve of people who lived in London, or, at worst, in Bath. More than anything I wanted a chance to study abroad, to properly confirm my right to the adjective 'educated'. I have since promised myself that I will attempt to write in Urdu at some point in my life.

By the time I realised what Urdu and the regional literatures of the subcontinent should have meant to me it was almost too late. I had already completed an MA in Modern English Literature at Reading University as a first step to acquiring a doctorate. It was after I had made a decision to work on W. B. Yeats' plays that it suddenly struck me that I should be working on Urdu literature, rather than English. I rang up Professor Russell, at

SOAS, wondering if he would accept me for postgraduate work on Ghalib. He wanted me to learn Persian first – it seemed too late to start learning a new language. I gave up and embarked on a much harder course: starting a family. My husband who had played along with a good grace and remarkable adaptability was relieved to think I was showing signs of settling down in London at last.

But when the children came, we were both overwhelmed. However, it was my life that changed more dramatically than his. No one prepares you properly either for the extremity of pain that the actual business of giving birth entails or for the enormous responsibility which parenthood brings. I had changed my status from Lecturer at Karachi University, an appointment that was offered to me the year I qualified, to that of a part-time student in England. Now I sank even lower to the rank of a full-time housewife. I felt wounded by that epithet, but that was how people saw me. I was no longer a person in my own right.

I tried to get part-time work. First, as a neighbourhood English teacher. I was short-listed but turned down by Brent Education Authority because I was 'over-qualified'. I felt crushed. The irony was that when I found paid work later it was not because of my English degree/s, but because I knew Urdu. Low status, low paid, part-time work for a survey company, it still gave me the self-esteem and what I most longed for, an identity other than that of mother and wife. I just needed to be a whole person again, for at least a few hours each week. I never contemplated full-time work because the moment I stepped out of the house I also felt utterly torn by guilt and neurotically anxious about my children. My brother's sudden death has left me with a legacy of anxiety about loved ones that is perhaps excessive.

It was almost eight years before I could consider a return to work. I did so when the youngest of my three children started school full time. This time I was not looking for a job. Dismayed by the Islamisation programme launched in Pakistan by General

Zia and alarmed by its implications for women I felt compelled to write about the status of women in Pakistan. Although I began to research the subject, I never wrote that book. What came out of that research and my personal anguish over the loss of work, self-esteem and identity that the combination of marriage and migration had precipitated was a new understanding of the mechanics of women's oppression and a much clearer insight into the links between race, class and gender. I became eager for immediate action. I campaigned at a few women's conferences and tried to write letters to newspapers and place articles on the issue.

I submitted my first article on the subject to *Asian Post*, a smart new magazine that was being published in London in those days. Chotu Karadia, the founder and editor, invited me to write regularly for them. I was delighted. Being paid for my writing meant I could view myself as a professional. One of my sisters pointed out to me that I needed the more persuasive and emotive language of fiction rather than that of research and scholarship if I really wanted to influence ideas and attitudes. Films rather than books were the medium to aim for – fair comment, of course, that helped me change direction.

I had only just started contributing regularly to the *Asian Post* when Ravinder Randhawa invited me to join a group she had set up. Supported by the GLC, the Asian Women Writers' Workshop used to meet at A Woman's Place under the arches of the railway bridge at the Embankment station. It was an exciting discovery – a group of women from the subcontinent who were all interested in writing, in feminist politics and in each other's work. Some of them became close friends and had a profound effect on me and my work. Most significantly on my sense of a distant but still valid national identity – until then I had entertained hopes of return. That possibility became more remote. It was only a partial renunciation of a former identity, as such renunciations usually are, and was certainly not based on the pragmatics of uniting behind the larger banner of Black women or of Asian women. It came when I genuinely began to *see* the limitations of thought and reach it imposed. I see it even now as a freedom earned through exile.

This was an awareness that crystallised further during the *Satanic Verses* row – oversimplified as it was by a polarisation around half-truths. I walked a tightrope between two realities – to both of which I felt seriously committed. The writer in me had every sympathy for Salman Rushdie whose novel had been turned into a political football, whose life had been placed in jeopardy (a sacrifice no writer should have to make) whilst the human being in me could also see the deep hurt of the community to which I had belonged. Ironically, many of the people who were attacking the book had not read it, just as the people who were defending it had not.

That growing alienation from the past was accentuated by the row – I had little desire left to return to Pakistan when that goalpost finally became attainable on a purely pragmatic level. The country had been forced to change – under General Zia – superficially but *visibly*. And the changes were deeply threatening to women, to the minorities and the dispossessed. I had changed perhaps even more. What I fear most is intolerance. Sentimental visits home were punctuated by heated and bitter political arguments with my nearest and dearest. Increasingly, I saw the shift in my connection with Pakistan as an émigrée. I was distancing myself from the mainstream Pakistani that I had been – and aligning myself with the oppressed. My woolly sympathy of the past had expanded to a much more acute understanding of the political structures that operated against the poor. This is a major concern of my writing now – a concern that crosses borders and feels the iniquities within societies and across frontiers, as much as it does on a worldwide basis between nations. Pakistan, or India or Britain, become merely the context for the scenario I choose for my work.

My life here has created a pervasive concern for minorities anywhere and everywhere. In Pakistan it had never even occurred to me that I was an 'Asian'. Asia is enormous, amorphous. In itself a majority. How can being an Asian hold

any meaning for anyone born on that continent? Here, I discovered I was an Asian. Lo and behold I began to feel 'Asian',
and more so, each year. As if it were something cumulative that
accrued around me, like the hardening shell of a crustacean. I
would feel my 'Asian woman' mask descend over me the
moment I stepped onto the tarmac at Heathrow. It worried me
initially – because of its ambassadorial implication – but, very
soon I realised that it also gave me a sort of anonymity and,
even more precious than that, a licence to be different. If you're
not part of the mainstream, I inferred, surely you have a right
to be weird and unpredictable? You can respond to injustice
with a tantrum and to road rage with a two-finger salute. On
quite a few occasions my father's fiery temper has surged into
my head without warning – and I have fought back, fearless
and unselfconscious in public situations – because someone has
been offensive or racist towards me.

I had already begun to take my writing quite seriously when
Jatinder Verma of Tara Arts invited me to a meeting and commissioned me to work on a devised play for the company. It
was a great way to be eased into a new genre. The production
earned me membership of the Writers' Guild – a very useful
validation of my work at an early stage in my writing career.
Tara Arts commissioned at least three other plays soon after that
and also constantly referred requests for theatre work from the
regions to me. Anyone looking for an Asian playwright would
get in touch. This work was building up an interesting writing
CV but fairly soon I realised that although I was constantly
writing, I rarely had a chance to initiate ideas of my own. Except
for my short fiction, all my work was paid for but was not what
I wanted to say. Here was the next pigeon-hole I had to fight.

One of the projects I initiated at this time was suggested by
a friend: a request for translations of contemporary feminist
poetry from Pakistan. Much of this material was new to me and
I was delighted to discover it. It took three years to collect the
poems and translate them, even longer to publish them here. It
brought me into contact with the women's movement in Paki-

stan and once again, I found new friends to cherish, amongst the writers, most specially Fahmida Riaz.

I had started teaching Creative Writing part time at an Adult Education Institute to supplement my income. Money was important for me to create more time for myself. When writing commissions became more regular I gave up the paid jobs to give myself more time to write. I became a co-founder of Kali Theatre Company which Rita Wolf had set up to produce one of my plays but this was almost by default. I did not want to commission myself – it felt too much like vanity publishing. I believed then I had hit the glass ceiling as far as theatre writing was concerned. I neglected its possibilities and decided to turn to fiction instead.

For two years my first novel hung in the balance with Virago's future whilst I continued to work on commissions for the stage and radio. I could not commence a new novel until it was published, nor had I been able to extricate myself from theatre and radio work. Its publication finally freed me to move on to my next book.

For a very long time I had believed that it would not be possible for me to write a novel because I could never capture my characters in English. I might not have attempted a novel in English had I not read Salman Rushdie's *Midnight's Children*. Rushdie had managed to subvert English for his own purpose. He not only transferred the linguistic patterns of Urdu quite uncannily into English, he also demonstrated a strategy for transposing rhythms and intonations from the subcontinent into it so successfully that it opened a door for me, as I am sure it did for many other writers whose lives were split across continents.

To this day the most painful question that I face about my writing in relation to my living in London is whether I would have been a different kind of writer if I had remained in Karachi, the city in which I was born. I know I would have written sooner or later. I also know that *success* as a writer would have come to me much faster and more easily over there. It would be less than honest though to now claim that I would have written only in Urdu – my association of five or six years with the English department of Karachi University had already nailed the coffin of that possibility long before my decision to settle abroad. Without a doubt it is not just your style, but also, the content of your work which is modified by the choice of the language in which you choose to write. I am sure I would have approached issues differently and written more about some experiences on which English imposes a silence.

Inevitably though, I would have been a different kind of person too. Hard to imagine how different? I feel a deep connection with my past that cannot be severed – even if I chose to exorcise it, that connection will survive in how others perceive me. That is easy to deduce from the treatment of writers whose work is deracinated to an extent and whose lives are distant from the real subcontinent. However, I know I myself don't want to sever my links with the past. It is the undoing and remaking of identity that has been the most transforming experience for me (besides motherhood, of course) and I do not know whether I would have grown as much as I have if I had not moved to Britain. To state the obvious: it is the moving itself that dictates the growth not the direction of the move. I have a suspicion that people who dig their roots too deep and refuse to be transplanted not only confine the choice of air they will breathe in, but, worse, lose the chance to find the space they might have found elsewhere to grow and spread out, unchecked by the strictures of the past.

On reflection I do not feel trapped by my identity/ies, past or present, or restricted by it/them. I use each when I want to. I am not enslaved by any of them. I have the ability to negotiate what I want from each. The knowledge that I can, like a chameleon, call upon one of several colours, side-step the preconceptions of others and survive in both worlds with a code that is not parochial or narrow in any sense but works like an unfailing talisman, on the whole is a fair return, I think, for the loss of a few certainties and a false sense of security that has fed on an unwillingness to change. Sadly, as always, the talisman comes with a condition. You have to surrender the right to belong.

G. V. Desani

❖❖❖❖❖❖❖❖❖❖❖❖❖❖❖❖

Liars, Hypocrites, Imperialists and Sages

G. V. Desani emerged into instant fame when, in 1948, his novel, *All About H. Hatterr* was published, and then – in 1958 – as abruptly disappeared again from public view.

An extraordinary, reeling, wild progress around India, it involved its hero (Hatterr) in a series of 'incidents' with a series of sages. But anyone going to *Hatterr* for a simple linear narrative will be grievously disappointed. The book's forte is the speedy fertility of its plotting and the disparity of its points of reference – from Shakespeare to Kipling, from the Vedas to the language of the mail-order catalogue. Emphatic, staccato, florid, opinionated and unpredictable, it re-invented English, and established *Hatterr* as a milestone on the road to Magic Realism. 'I write rigmarole English, staining your goodly, godly tongue, maybe,' says Hatterr. But, 'it is the language that makes the book, a sort of creative chaos that grumbles at restraining banks,' says Anthony Burgess in his Introduction to the book.

The piece that follows is drawn from taped interviews with Desani, rediscovered in retirement in Texas where he had been Professor of Philosophy, a post that he took on in accordance with Theravadin vows to take everything offered and not to let his ego intervene. An octogenarian and with failing sight, he still communicates the sense of audacity and independence that readers will recognise from his influential novel of four decades ago.

Shikarpur, in the province of Sind, was the city my father
belonged to. 'Shikar' means hunt; 'pur' means town: Town
of the Hunt, where the kings went to hunt. These people were,
with utmost respect – I ought to have some respect for them –
liars. They were classes of people. Some of them were just
travellers, merchants. That means that they have, for a very long
time in Indian history, travelled.

My people were merchants. Not merchants, really, they were
just adventurers trying to look around for anything they could
find to start a business. Business was usually done through
middlemen. Third parties, called brokers. So if a man could not
start in any business or anything to make a living, he would
become a broker, a middleman. He would negotiate. His com-
petence was language. He would talk, persuade people, buy
and sell on your behalf. That is what Shikarpur people were
doing. As a people we didn't like each other. This was a small
town.

If anybody could not succeed in anything, brokerage
included, they sent them abroad. They had built up a myth of
their superiority to the other people: they were savages, lower.

They went to Africa. It was on the coast of the Arabian sea.
You get an Arab dhow (Arab ship with sails) to Arabia, then
from Arabia to Africa. My father was one of the fellows who
landed in Africa. He took his family with him, of course, because
they said, 'We want our Indian cooking'. This is an affliction up
till now, addiction to cooking. I don't know whether I can say
addiction to food. It's a necessity. But they didn't know anything
about nutrition, and so on. They take their women with them
for cooking. (They had grave objection to displaying their
women, their faces. This is not a Hindu idea. Muslim culture
brought Purdah, 'Purdah' means veil, to hide their women.)
They were not good cooks, not at all.

(It might interest some people: there is no such word as
'Hindu'. This is preposterous, not mentioned in the Indian
books. It was Iranian inability to pronounce the letter 's' that

made Sapta Sindhu, a province of India at that time, Seven Sindus, Seven Rivers, into Hapta Hindus.)

It was easy to succeed in Africa at that time because people were backward and all you had to do was steal from them. I am being truthful. It is a correct word. My father established himself in a place which my friend Mr Sean Mandy, an Irish gentleman and the editor of a paper, told me was heaven on earth. Beauty, not far from the Abyssinian Highlands. He had lived there, too.

The port was Mombasa. I remember it. I remember the sea. My attraction to waters was due to this image of Mombasa, which was blue sea with foam on it, white and blue. And, of course, the scene there, when you arrived in Mombasa was so strange, that I had to use my imagination, to think about strange places, which were not real.

I was born in Nairobi, East Africa, which was about a night's run by train from Mombasa. The train was being built when my father arrived. What did he do? He went into the fuel business. Wood was the only source of fuel with which you could heat the houses or cook. He would bid for land, small jungle growth, then employ Africans. They would chop the wood into small pieces, and these were for sale.

He had a store – as most Indians did – a small store in which you could get anything at sale. We had about a hundred people employed at a time. He used to have an iron pot boiling and in it you'd throw some grain, whatever grain you had. This used to boil all the time. They would dip it out with chips of wood. No bowls or spoons. They would lick it up from this piece of wood. Can't keep it on the tongue very long because it will burn. It was boiling hot. That is all the wages they got. To eat. They were living on this grain broth. They couldn't compete, couldn't share my father's profits on selling this wood. And they did all the work. He did well, by his standards.

We had animals, particularly lions, who were declared to be man-eaters. I had two cousins eaten alive in bed.

This was a very small society. I have no recollection of the language, not more than sixty words of an African dialect. I learned it from my nurse. She was a Kikuyu tribeswoman. It was my first language, then Sindhi.

My father returned to Sind to marry off his daughters. I have a definite date to go by, the day of Armistice, First World War. The school will be closed, it will be a day of celebration. This was a British victory. That's what we were supposed to celebrate. We had, of course, no interest whatsoever.

We arrived in the city of Karachi by ship, through the Arabian Sea. It was the capital of Sind, on the Indus River. (There are references in Indian history of an Indus valley civilisation. The subject bores me. Except curious pieces, such as, they knew underground drainage at a time unheard of in Europe.)

The people of Shikarpur, of whom I can speak briefly, but not very respectfully, struck me as an entity. These cities had an individualism of some sort. Lying. That's correct. The term belongs, of course, to ethics. It's a wrong thing. We didn't know about it. It was called being clever, smart. How would they lie? We are sixty-five thousand people in that city. For no reason at all, they started saying, 'We are a hundred thousand'.

It's called a bluff: I questioned them that there is no record that they were a hundred thousand. A moneylender, he calls himself a banker. Nobody taught them that it's an untruth. You cannot make histories, you cannot write books without order. They had no respect for it.

Then we had no street lighting. It came in due course in Karachi. They were using obscenities. What we would like to do to Karachi's – that is the city we were envying – mother. I don't think it is in good taste – I'm not sure if it is legal – to translate these words. May I bed Karachi's mother. We are going to get lamps soon.

As soon as the street lighting came, the whole city just went crazy. They were meeting each other under the street lamps. That was a meeting place. There is no need to go to Karachi. We have a city as good as Karachi. From two street lamps.

My father was a very difficult man. I'm trying to be polite to his memory. He was a typical Shikarpuri. His orders were: the Hindu religion, so-called Hindu religion, had prescribed that your elders are God, or at least so he rendered it. So my father had adopted that particular advantageous position, in which case, every male child was preferred progeny to have, not girls. (Women were denied reading books, like the Vedas, the oldest books.)

I had a very grave dispute with my father. We disagreed on a way of life of Indians and British, and others. He, a Hindu, held enmity against the principal community, Muslims, who had ruled Sind before the British. There is a traditional enmity between these two groups. Islam is a good religion; I have nothing against it. My father told me not to use the word Christian, or Islam, in the house.

'What shall I use?' I asked him.

He told me to say, 'I have blackened my face.' It means I have disgraced my family by consorting with Muslims, Christians. Christians and Muslims had very uncomplimentary words for Hindus, too.

One of the ways of life in which we differed were child marriages. My father was very keen on it. I did not know all the mechanisms of these, successful or unsuccessful, child marriages. We had no voice in them. Now, at my age, fourteen years, my father said, 'I've given my word.' When I refused, he told me, 'You will go to hell.' There's a very ugly word for it, 'Naraka', in Sanskrit. It amounts to a curse. You mustn't say that to anybody, but he told me to my face, 'You'll go to Naraka!' I asked him, 'Why?' Now, this is not permitted, to question your father. He told me, 'Because you don't obey your father. It's our religion.'

Obeying the father was to live like him. One of the conditions was to accept child marriage with a girl who was eight years old. We were actually, without using mincing words, robbing her. The money that her parents, grandparents had collected to see that she could live a free person – second marriage was not allowed in India. Well-known fact, child marriages. Husband dies after one year, they have no son, no husband. They are left on society; in fear all the time. They are nobody. The life ends there. So they had made a collection, a sum of money for her. My father wanted that money as dowry. That was the chief incentive: greed. This can better be explained in religious terms, Christian terms. Paul said the root of all evil is love of money. It was a very considered remark.

He gave me an ultimatum. Marry the girl before I turned sixteen, or he would disown me. I ran away from home. Third time, I made it to London. Disowned. No money. I had no English.

Two years I was in London. I didn't have a fire for two years. Extremely cold. A man told me, 'Why do you go about without a coat?' I didn't understand him, that he meant an overcoat. 'You will run into trouble: pneumonia.' Truly, my first year in London I did not know the meaning of the word pneumonia. What does it mean? No language. I learned to put newspapers under my shirt.

I found a friend, Mr Greenwood, who introduced me to the Bible. He was about seventy-one and I was not sixteen at that time. He helped me to learn English. Tried to give me a craft, repairing watches, which I could market – I didn't develop any. We remained friends for a long time.

I had, meanwhile, come across books of the Rationalist Association. Bertrand Russell was one of the contributors. I got acquainted with his views, and other scientists. They were questioning everything, Genesis, from the Bible; the concept of God. It questioned people, 'When you say, "I will go to heaven," where is heaven? Have you seen a person come back, descend from heaven?' From original analysis of things it turned to the way we should live. It was an attack on religion. They were anti-Christian, as I understood the Bible.

It was to me like being in daylight after Indian superstition about Deity and speculation. I was most impressed. Felt free as it were. I am grateful to this illumination.

In Bombay, I had heard about some books written by sages,

hand-written texts on palm leaf, which were available only in south India, in Tamil, a South Indian language. These were termed 'Nadi' texts. They were supposed to demonstrate the extraordinary powers of very renowned sages. Somebody told me I'd find my name described in the book.

I sought out a reader, who had one of these books. It gave my name and my parents' names. It said I was born in East Africa, Nairobi, in nineteen hundred and eight. All correct.

These texts told me personally, under my name, that he will not have any marketable skills, something that I could turn into money, such as a petty skill. I was surprised that anybody should know this. It told me, he will write books of status.

Next, because I was not very friendly as a young person – like to be alone and don't want to make friends, commitments – it also told me that he will need some people to raise him up. Indeed, I did need people to raise me up.

The sage saw that. That was his power.

He told me, 'People who would raise him up would belong in another country. They would have served their country so well that their government would have honoured them, they would raise him up.'

I didn't know what it means. I looked at it up, down. Can it mean this group? No group there. I was not in England, even, where I might meet them. He didn't mention which country.

This was my first acquaintance with power, with real power which some people do develop, power which these Rationalist Association books couldn't provide. They had verbal skills. They had logic to play with. These texts, for the first time, gave me evidence that books about speculation about God, against Christianity, and so on, were verbal feats. Words. Clever people – you have to equip yourself for years to argue with them.

These texts are religious books; they are also books of prophecy. Prophecy, as a reality, has been admitted in the Bible. Of Christ's attitude to Judas: he's not responsible. He said that crucifixion is not in the hands of any person but from the Lord on high. This was his destiny, Judas' destiny.

I simultaneously read a statement like that from Guru Nanak, Guru of Sikhs, a very spiritual man. He said, 'Not a leaf stirs without the order from the great God.' These are real experiences. Inevitability. I connected some of these things to Indian texts. That influenced me.

(The Sikhs are Hindus. Their last Guru, Govind Singh, told them that your duty is to drive out Islam from India. How do you do that? You first wear beards so that you can mix with these foreigners and appear as one of them. He gave them certain marks they should wear, including hidden daggers. Mix with them. When you have an opportunity, cut their throats. They take their name from the word, siksha. Sikshas are students, disciples. Singh means lion. It's quite absurd, if you have about ten people in your household and each calling themselves So-and-so Lion, So-and-so Lion. We are ridiculous, but we didn't have any sense of humour about our particular way of life.)

I could not visualise that I would be in England, to be helped by these gentlemen. I named them. One of them was the Marquess of Zetland, K. G., P. C. Lord Zetland. I couldn't visualise what Lord Zetland has to do with me. He was a Governor of Bengal. I remember I was asked to lecture at the Mahabodhi Society in Calcutta. We were getting a relic of Gautama, the Buddha. There's a crowd in the street. I saw it from my hotel room. Lord Zetland took off his hat and his shoes – that's a humble posture – and joined the monks and carried the relic on his head. That endeared him to the Indian Buddhist population – and to me, too, of course. He had also written a book that influenced me. It was called *Heart of the Aryavartha*. That's an ancient name of India, home of the Aryas – the word 'arya' was being used long before Germans had heard about it. (I remember being very irritated with some of my professor friends, not having looked at this book.) He was a national trustee of all the treasures of England, British Museum included. He had said of me, about fifteen years before, that I will be an interpreter between East and West, to interpret our culture to them and their culture to us.

I arrived in England. The war had about begun. My reasons for being in England at that time, in spite of the suggestions made by everybody I knew, I did it because I just wanted to know what war is like. How much changes it makes in human nature, in day-to-day people. Curiosity.

I met Sir Lancelot Graham. He told me, 'I would have some claim to be a Sindhi too.' He was the Governor of Sind. 'I've heard so much about you from my friend, Sir Harry Lindsay, Director of the Imperial Institute. Would you please come for tea?'

I met him for tea. I asked him, 'Sir Lancelot, what are you doing here?' I had this recollection of the prediction. He said that, 'We are here to help the old country.' They were there: governors of Bengal, governors of Sind, all kind of high officials. Declined to accept the salaries which were due to them for imperial preference.

All came to England to help the old country, to serve. Free. As we talked, I gradually began to recognise that it might be referring to these civil servants, with whom I had very little to do in the normal course of life.

The Ministry of Information said, 'Do you know Mr Graham?'
'I do.'
'There is a debate. He's supporting the position that the Indian political reforms are premature. Will you oppose it?'
'I'll oppose it.'

All my friends told me not to risk having a skirmish with him. Foregone conclusion. He'll sweep the floor with you. Because of his awe-inspiring credentials, lawyer, first-class first, barrister, and Secretary of Indian Legislative Assembly for ten years. Twice Governor of provinces. Two knighthoods. Every law at his fingertips.

He naturally took a point which was successful, which was that we have treaties with the Indian Princes. Great segments of earth in India belonged to Indian Princes. They were not defeated in wars like Rajputs, or others, but they agreed to become part of the British Empire. They helped Britain in numbers of population – workers, soldiers – particularly Rajputs. Recruitments were done in martial races – so called. People who had a caste for warriors. And we had treaties with them. It's not an honourable thing to go back on your treaties: that was his point. And, of course, he was applauded. We cannot just walk out of India and say to these friends, 'You look after your own interests'. We have signed papers to say we'll come to your rescue.

At that time, the most important news in India was a private quarrel between an India Raja and a young woman. She broke with him. The Raja issued an order. About ten people broke into her house. A woman living alone in India; they made about fifty cuts on her face, to ruin her physical beauty. That was a terrible attack, but the police wouldn't take a report because they are forbidden by law to act, to inquire against the Rajas.

In this treaty he had special rights. And here was Sir Lancelot Graham asking me to believe that it was also a matter of honour of the British people, to honour those rights. I found it very difficult to agree to it. I said so. In the end, the audience were with me. We prevailed.

I defeated him. Forty votes to seven. That's seven to Graham, not me. His defeat was so spectacular, it might have raised me up exactly as they said. He told me with utmost contempt – I didn't know he had such contempt for English people, his people – he said, 'You don't want to follow these riff-raffs.' They were British administrators and others who had come to see the debate, and there were Indians, too.

'What shall I do?' I asked him.

'Get into the House,' he said. He gave me a quotation from Kipling, 'When strong men meet each other, from ends of the earth, they recognise each other.'

I told him, 'I haven't got the means to stand for Parliament.'

He said, 'We'd look after all that.' He took me to his club – the whole damned hoax, just between four people talking together, they give you a safe seat. That's how it was done. He said, 'You stand up and use your powers of speech,' he told me, 'of eloquence, and defeat them and you'll become a person.' I told him, 'I'm writing this book, *H. Hatterr*. I brought two copies for you.'

And where was he travelling? A function in honour of Montgomery. He was as big a name as the German general, you know, Rommel. 'Do you know him?' He said, 'Yes, he was my fag.'

'Fag' means servant in public school, Rugby School. For years, they clean up your urine and other things in the morning. They train them that way. He also told me, 'Here are your books. I made a rule. I never take a friend's book with inscription. I buy their books, if I'm a friend.' So he bought two copies, one for Montgomery, one for himself. He didn't know his school, his Rugby School, was described in such common terms. He daren't show it to Montgomery. It's their God, you see. Then he told me, very affectionately, 'You scoundrel. You didn't tell me!'

It was to his credit Sir Lancelot didn't hold it against me. He simply took me to dinner and we were friends for many years, until his death in England.

He was my patron in England, exactly as the book said. Then others did.

In conversation one evening, Prof. Edmund Blunden mentioned, 'This is an age of mediocre poets.' He's a poet himself and his book, *Undertones of War*, was the most discussed book of World War One. I told him, 'I will add to it.' Now, he didn't think that this remark was strictly appropriate. We were talking about great writers. They're not here. Then, in my introduction he wrote, 'He's a dreamer.' After great thought, I imagine. Dreamers are people who just imagine fits of grandeur. After I showed him some Shakespearean quotations, he told me he couldn't find them in a concordance anywhere. 'Where are they?' I told him, 'I wrote them.' This so shakened him that he added the phrase, 'What if dreams prove true?' But not all such persons are as conscientious.

Mr Eric Blair (George Orwell) at that time hadn't published his book, *Animal Farm*, which became a success in America. At that time the cold war between America and Russia was not over. Mr Orwell had a series of books he was talking about on the BBC, where he was a producer, on the programme, *Books That Changed The World*.

He asked me if I could pick an Indian book to add to it. He told me, 'You can look in my office and I'll show you the file, what other people have said.' I was astonished that there were about four or five authors who were ruling us, whose thought was ruling us. The rest don't matter at all. The founder of Christianity, the founder of Islam, the Buddha.

I introduced the *Bhagavad Gita*, Song of the Lord, which is a religious classic. I have seen readers of it in every country. This religion does not hold God responsible for our miseries, but ourselves. The thing is that deeds we have forgotten, they have got to be atoned for. How do you atone for it? By serving God's purposes. God does not punish us for our deeds. Who does? We do, they say. It's our karma. (Unfortunately in India it's been reduced into feeding about four Brahmins a meal once a year in the name of your ancestors.)

This book consoles me often. The discoverer of Lhasa, Sir Francis Younghusband, told me many times he despairs of human enterprises, where it is all going to end. And he told me this particular verse in the *Bhagavad Gita*, 'Whenever righteousness is on the decline, I will come on earth,' has means of consolation to him.

'What is the meaning of karma,' George Orwell asked me, 'What does it mean?' Quite a legitimate question. People don't think they need to have a definition of karma, which means simply, action. How do you explain it? But of course, it does need instruction, because it's something to discipline oneself to do right action. So I asked him, 'My dear fellow, when I came to see you' – I knew him well enough for that – 'what were you doing here in the BBC office, Oxford Street office?' He said, 'I was cursing the weather.' 'That is karma.' Of course, he wanted to object. He said, 'Damn it, I'm not cursing any individual or having any ill will for any person.'

But, karma is, according to the *Bhagavad Gita*, three-fold. Mental, that is what you were doing, mental karma. Sitting there and holding thoughts tinged with anger and hatred, against people or weather. It doesn't matter what you are against, it's a scheme of evil: that you do bad karma through mind. Buddhists, too – later tradition. Or, if it is not mental karma, then verbal – words of hatred. Then physical action, karma. That would inflame your particular consciousness. That's the karma. Doesn't matter whether it's weather or anything.

What does it mean in actual practice? It means, experts have told us, if you are born again, emerge again, then that would be the child of the earlier mental state. An angry person is a bad candidate for human birth. These are real problems.

There are some people I've known, children particularly, too, they walk through a room and they change it. They don't live there but simply being present. During the war I have known people in London, children terrified of the sounds, screams of bombs. And then I've gathered them into my arms and told them to hold on to me, tight, to my neck. And their presence at that time had given me almost a spiritual experience of being a father to little people. This couldn't be had otherwise, without them. There was something about them I have not quite understood, emanations from their bodies.

So, these things happen that give me faith, to believe in extra intervention in our favour if we are doing a good deed, then we are on the good side. Good forces help us. If we are on the bad side then bad forces help us. Or not help us, either way.

From Sir Lancelot, right up to Lord Zetland, they helped me all the way, including being appointed as a spokesman for the British Government – lecturer for the Ministry of Information. My subjects were Indian culture, heritage, etc. Incidentally, I pointed out that the present India was not following those traditions – a religious protest.

Next is to illuminate people. What will happen if Rommel

went about two inches outside the borders of Egypt towards India? The rumours will say, 'British are on the run. The war will end very soon.'

These lectures really were to businessmen, luncheon hours. They didn't know these issues. So the Ministry used to send me to these people. There were specialised requests also. If the Western culture has affected any of the Indian religion. Questions like these were asked from Harrow School. I answered those questions.

Now, this was a proof of real power, not power I came across through the Rationalist Association's treatment of religion, Indian superstition, dirty water, Ganges.

I published a book. Which was the most discussed book of the year according to some magazine, monthly magazine. I had admirers like Mr T. S. Eliot, who had interceded to allow publication, E. M. Forster, and others. It attracted attention in India, too.

So, that way the years had passed and at the end of the war I thought I'll go back to India, and I made for India. Years in jungles, in monasteries. I haven't got patience or time to look up the years or the dates. I do not care about these details. I have cared about them intensely in my younger days.

There wasn't a single problem in India that I saw, no matter how exotic it looked, which had not arisen in Europe, sometime or the other. You only have to read the novelists, Victorian, and others. Same problems were there, including plague, when it was not identified or traced to rats. They solved them by the scientific method. Economic and other problems were faced in Europe. All these problems had been dealt with very ably.

And here I am. And my reputation abroad led to the US Government inviting me here as a lecturer, Senator Fulbright exchange visitor, then Professor of Philosophy at the University of Texas. I've stayed here since.

I intend to write two books as a religious duty, above all else, because it is prophesied for me and ordered for me, 'That's your purpose in life.' Rightly or wrongly, I've accepted this. First will be about my life. I haven't told you enough about my follies; we are growing up and learning. And next, about these Nadi texts. There weren't many mistakes in their predictions.

I am looking at the Bible these days because I am going to address Christians sooner or later. I asked a young friend to read to me because I have difficulty in reading. St John's gospel. But we have an important message. And it is a message which religion gives, Christianity gives, Gautama the Buddha gives. So we will hope to convert nobody. I merely wish to confide in you as friends. That is the purpose of these talks. This knowledge was so new to me. I hope it is new to you, too.

Homi Bhabha

❖❖❖❖❖❖❖❖❖❖❖❖❖❖❖❖❖

The Vernacular Cosmopolitan

Homi Bhabha is widely known and greatly respected as an international cultural theorist, 'A reader of enormous subtlety and wit, a theorist of uncommon power. His work is a landmark of the exchange between ages, genres and cultures; the colonial, post-colonial, modernist and post-modernist,' said Edward Said. His piece here demonstrates something insufficiently noted – the way in which his creative imagination informs his acute thought.

Homi Bhabha draws on a vivid range of sympathies – poetry and the visual arts, as well as his passionate engagement with the redefinition of identity that is part of the canon of post-modernism. His approach has helped to ground the developments taking place in overtly creative fiction by placing them within a challenging and thought-provoking critical framework.

Homi Bhabha is the Chester D Tripp Distinguished Professor in the Humanities, Departments of English, Art and South Asia, at the University of Chicago and Visiting Professor at University College, London. His publications include *Nation and Narration* (Routledge, 1990) and *The Location of Culture* (Routledge, 1994).

Mendelssohn is not a peak, but a plateau.

His Englishness.   Wittgenstein, *Culture and Value*

I am not quite midnight's child, having missed my tryst with India's historic destiny by a few years. But great events persist beyond their happening, leaving a sense of expectation in the air like the telling vacancy of weather that follows a spectacular storm, never letting you forget that it occurred. My childhood was filled with accounts of India's struggle for Independence, its complex histories of cultures – British, Hindu, Muslim – caught in that deadly embrace of imperial power and domination that never fails to produce its uncomfortable residues of enmity and amity, love and hate. In a small way, my own life was caught on the crossroads that marked the end of empire, with its push towards the new horizons of a Third World of free nations, and, in the opposite direction, a pull from the past, a power exerted by the art and literature of Europe, that was so much a part of the anglicised world of the post-colonial Indian bourgeoisie. During my young adulthood in Bombay I never imagined that I would live elsewhere; like my relatives who went abroad for their further education, I was sure that I would return home to live, to fall back into a pattern of habits and relationships that I greatly valued. A quarter of a century later, as I begin to write this essay, my life divided between Britain and America, I cannot imagine returning to live permanently in India. But what is even more surprising is that I cannot imagine what it would be like to live without that unresolved tension between cultures and countries that has become the narrative of my life, and the defining characteristic of my work.

All this was brought home to me in a graphic way when I took part in a BBC Radio programme devoted to India's 50th Anniversary of Independence. The scene in the studio resembled a stage set for the problem of cultural displacement that I have just described. Five South Asians of Indian or Pakistani descent, in different stages of expatriation, trying to wrest control of those divine and demoniac twins, India and Pakistan, born together from a cleft womb, still as restless as the day they emerged into the harsh light of nationhood. We were a gathering of stragglers seemingly adept at making exits and entrances, but not without our enduring passions and interests: two Pakistani academics, involved in writing the history of their nation, living and working in Cambridge and New York; a writer of vivid

Indian historical fictions splitting her life between New York, London and Delhi; a film maker, equally at home in New York, Bombay and London, whose elegant recreations of English and American literary classics have helped a generation of viewers to inhabit their literary heritage with the ease of visiting a listed house or touring a great, ornamental park. And then there was me, a literary critic teaching at an American university, moving between Chicago and London, and returning annually to my family home in Bombay to replenish those hungers, and revisit those doubts, that haunt the place of childhood. What gives us the authority to speak? Caught between worlds that collide as often as they collude, are we representative of anything but ourselves?

I have asked myself these questions at different times throughout my life. They are neither intrusive nor indulgent, nor are they peculiar to the experience of migration. Such self-probing reflects my experience of belonging to the Parsi middle classes, the most Western and bourgeois of Indian minorities – doctors, lawyers, architects, industrialists, entrepreneurs, a few academics. Being a Parsi, without any originary link to the major Hindu or Muslim traditions was, for some people, a betrayal in itself: a hybrid, a half-breed, a foot in each camp and groundless for all that. Such questions and doubts recurred when I set out from Bombay, in the seventies, to study English at Oxford. My coming to England was, in many ways, the culmination of a middle-class trajectory where formal education and 'high' culture consisted largely in emulating the canons of English taste and conforming to its civilisational customs and comforts. However, my everyday life was lived in that rich cultural mix of languages and lifestyles that most cosmopolitan Indian cities celebrate and perpetuate – 'Bombay' Hindustani, 'Parsi' Gujarati, mongrel Marathi – all held in a suspension of Welsh-missionary accented, sing-song English peppered with an anglo-Indian *patois* that was, at times, cast aside for American slang picked up from the movies or popular music. The English Language, at times, had the archaic feel of throwing open an antique carved almirah to find yourself engulfed in the faded smell of mothballs and beautiful brittle linens; at other times it had the mix-and-match quality of a movable feast, like Bombay street-food, spicy, cheap, available in all kinds of quantities and combinations, delicious as much for its flavours as its dangers – unhygienic, probably infectious, quite insanitary. I went to Oxford to embellish the antique charms of the almirah; I ended up realising how much I desired street-food.

My sense of 'Englishness' resembled a chest that preserved the foreignness of somebody's past, but was now forced to accommodate the messy but vital bric-à-brac of a quite 'other' present. Soon, I was to encounter this 'cupboard' feeling for real. My college bedroom, at Oxford, was the size of a closet, dominated by a handsome old chest whose loosely hinged doors had to be held back before you could make your way in, or firmly closed before you could let yourself out. Only now do I realise that this ambivalent sense of enclosure and exclusion was symbolic of my anxious entry into British cultural life. I felt constrained by college rules, isolated by the predictable town and gown divide, bereft of a conversation in many languages, the smell of ground spices, *masalas*, roasting at mealtimes, the sunset hour when the heat is sucked up by the lifting sea breeze as the tide comes in. I was living out a dream that many middle-class Indians would aspire to, and yet, in the middle of it all, I was both engrossed and unsurprised.

There is a great subtlety in this old England of ours: shades of meaning and degrees of cultural distinction seem to flow into each other like a range of old hills disappearing, fold upon fold, into the unseeable distance. You stumble upon a social landscape where the merest tremor of a tone, a vowel flattened or faltering, reveals a whole geography of belonging – class, region, family, education. For an apprentice literary critic from Bombay, who once had to imagine an entire cultural landscape in which to locate the 'Englishness' of literature, there was suddenly a new-found freedom. Jane Austen's ironies came alive, and the ellipses in Virginia Woolf's prose started to speak. I was fascinated but unmoved. Why was I intellectually unfulfilled when I found myself in the very midst of the literary culture that I had chosen to follow?

Fumbling towards an answer to that question brings me closer to the most important lesson that I was to learn in my early years in England. It was this: what one expects to find at the very *centre* of life or literature may only be the dream of the deprived and the powerless; the centre may be most interesting in its elusiveness, as the enigma of authority. What was missing from the world of English literary study was a rich and provocative encounter with the pertinence of what lay in an *oblique* relation to the forces of centering. This is not, in any sense, to sanctify the marginal, but to realise – to make graphic – what it means to survive, to produce, to labour, create one's own imaginative world within a world system whose major impulses and investments are pointed in a direction away from you. There is a lesson in that neglect that takes you, at times, beyond and *behind* the great narratives of centre and periphery. Remember the awful realisation endured by Rahul Singh, V. S. Naipaul's mimic man, when it began to dawn on him that the great stone walls of London didn't contain a unique weight and resonance; *they* were like stones elsewhere and everywhere, other stones were not pale shadows of them.

My need to have my transitional, extraterritorial existence acknowledged would not have been fulfilled by a critical tradition 'owning up' to its imperial 'past', like a fact held in the aspic of the archive. I was searching for an active understanding of the living relationship, the unceasing movement, *in between* colony and metropole, recognised in its most awkward and awesome juxtapositions. John Stuart Mill, for instance, who worked for the India Office realised that one of the major conundrums of his theory of liberty consisted in the fact that he was a democrat in his country and a despot in another's land. For the canons of British literary culture to take responsibility for such a double or forked ancestry requires a revisionary estimate of liberalism as an ideology of conquest, or an instru-

Homi Bhabha

ment in the cultural of assimilation. What has to be acknowledged – as Mill *almost* did – is that the self-contradictoriness of liberalism is an unwinnable war raging in its heart between 'universalism' as a principle of cultural comparison, and ethnocentricism as a condition of judgement. It is this working contradiction between the epistemological and the ethical, between description and judgement, that produces a strategy of 'liberal' containment in situations of cultural conflict. It can also be an inner war that is unsustainable.

Such, I believe, is E. M. Forster's insight into the colonial career of the liberal idea which has a marked relevance for our times too. In *A Passage to India* he explores the flailing of liberalism's great mission of tolerance and accommodation when, in the anxious politics of empire, racial difference and sexual desire raise their heads and all around them lose theirs. The great lesson that Forster's book teaches is that it is the closeness or proximity of 'cultural' differences, not the vast gaps between nations and peoples, that is the most critical and crisis-laden area of communication. Aziz and Adela were trying to create a new medium of understanding that would make it irrelevant for them to retreat to the certitudes of their own cultural foundations, and it is for this reason that Forster leads them into the darkness of the Marabar Caves. There, prior assumptions and prejudices are flung into the void and, for a spare moment, the colonial mehmsahib and the educated native confront each other through a glass darkly . . . not seeking their own reflections, but the possibility of a proximate existence.

Coming from India where foreigners are warmly invited into the fold, even fetishised for their 'foreignness', the ethic of proximity remains for me an essential quality of communality. It was a shock to be aggressively asked by a number of hideous men with red faces and bad teeth, 'When d'ya row yourself ashore?'. Landladies had mysteriously found tenants in the few minutes between a telephone inquiry and one's turning up on the doorstep. But these were minor inconveniences when compared to those whose homes were fire-bombed, whose children maimed,

138 ❖

who stood for half a lifetime in dole queues or waited almost as long for entry visas to allow migrant families to be united in the UK. When I hear the familiar complaint 'they're taking our jobs' or 'the government's soft on these foreign scroungers', I never quite believe that it is adequate to deplore the sentiment, and then proceed to 'understand' the racist reaction as a form of White working-class protest against the dismantling of the Welfare State. Every time I hear, 'Paki go home!' I sense deep fear and resentment on the part of the racist – whether he is White or Black – at the spectacle of the *survival* of migrants and minorities; their ability to lead lives that are part of a recognisable and shared sense of civic virtue while maintaining their cultural differences, their language, food, festivals, religious customs.

It is this double life of British minorities that makes them 'vernacular cosmopolitans', translating between cultures, renegotiating traditions from a position where 'locality' insists on its own terms, while entering into larger national and societal conversations. This is not a cosmopolitanism of the élite variety inspired by universalist patterns of humanistic thought that run gloriously across cultures, establishing an enlightened unity. Vernacular cosmopolitans are compelled to make a tryst with cultural translation as an act of survival. Their specific and local histories, often threatened and repressed, are inserted 'between the lines' of dominant cultural practices.

To occupy such an 'in-between' space is often the result of oppression and inequality. Those who occupy marginal or minority positions within cultures and societies often have no option but to occupy such interstitial spaces. Yet, there is a lesson to be learned from such cramped conditions of cultural creativity. From the perspective of the 'in-between', claims to cultural authenticity and sovereignty – supremacy, autonomy, hierarchy – are less significant 'values' than an awareness of the hybrid conditions of inter-cultural exchange. Aesthetic and ethical values are derived from those boundaries *between* languages, territories and communities that belong, strictly speaking, to no one culture; these are values produced in the on-going practices and performances of 'crossing over', and become meaningful as cultures to the extent to which they are intricately and intimately interleaved with one another.

My own working life as a literary critic has entailed a similar process of finding my voice in-between the lines of other people's texts, in a form of translation analogous to the process I have just described. My search for a subject of my own did not emerge directly from the English authors that I avidly read, nor from the Indian writers with whom I deeply identified; it was the Indo-Caribbean world of V. S. Naipaul, which I neither knew nor particularly cared about, that was to become the diversionary, exilic route that led me to the historical themes and theoretical questions that were to form the core of my thinking. For reasons still obscure to me, it was the detour through Naipaul's *milieu* that brought back the world of post-colonial India to me, even as Naipaul himself took a more direct route from Trinidad back to his ancestral home in India, in order to seek out a deeper understanding of the 'shipwrecked' lives of the Hindu indentured community to which he belonged. *A House for Mr Biswas, The Mimic Men, In a Free State*, these novels have been celebrated for achieving a cast of characters whose unpromising lives were turned, by Naipaul, into the most memorable portraits of individuals striving for their independence, establishing their autonomy, against all the odds. My identification with Naipaul's writing was less concerned with the triumph of the human spirit. I was more intrigued by the ability of his characters to make their way in the world acknowledging its fragmented structure, its split imperatives, its sense of an absence of authority. In Naipaul's view, of course, this was nothing more than the 'wretched' condition of the Caribbean, and his unrelenting irony and despair about the islands lead him to conservative conclusions. My own view was different: the ability of his characters to forebear their despair, to work through their anxieties and alienations towards a life that is radically incomplete and yet intricately communitarian, busy with activity, noisy with stories, garrulous with grotesquerie, gossip, humour, aspirations, fantasies – these are signs of a culture of survival that emerges from the other side of the colonial enterprise, the darker side. Naipaul's people are less remarkable for their portrayal of literary 'character' than for the possibilities of personhood they symbolise – a way of being in the world that resists the tragical view, held by many, that the colonised are peoples without a history. Armed with a comedic spirit of persistence, Naipaul's characters reveal, in the midst of loss, poverty and defeat, the chances for creativity, humour and the virtues of a common life enshrined in the everyday experience of social marginality – a common life that is not in the least commonplace.

Naipaul's people exceed the traditions within which they find themselves constrained, transgress the languages of conformity that they inherit, unsettle the colonial and post-colonial preconceptions of their precarious lives. They too are vernacular cosmopolitans – although often obsessed by their provinciality – moving in-between cultural traditions and revealing hybrid forms of life and art that do not have a prior existence within the discrete world of any single culture or language. Cultural translation is not simply appropriation or adaptation; it is a process through which cultures are required to revise their own systems of reference, norms and values, by departing from their habitual or 'inbred' rules of transformation. Ambivalence and antagonism accompanies any act of cultural translation, because negotiating with the 'difference of the other' reveals the radical insufficiency of sedimented, settled systems of meaning and signification; it demonstrates, as well, the inadequacy of those 'structures of feeling' (as Raymond Williams would have put it), through which we experience our cultural authenticity and authority as being somehow 'natural' to us and part of a national landscape.

From the mid-eighties onwards, I sensed a change in the cultural scene. As the Tories marched triumphant and the Labour Party recoiled from the horror of its own increasing irrelevance, left and right seemed to meet in an unholy alliance. There was a sense of drift and directionlessness, and in that unpromising moment the arts of Britain's 'Black' communities developed a marked resonance and relevance. The landscape with which I opened – subtle social shifts and folds harbouring fixed hierarchies and enclosed conventions – became less significant for me. The common grounds of everyday life were slowly changing, at least from where I stood, and so was the weather. The most lasting image of this transformation is to be found in *The Satanic Verses* where the vibrancy and insurgency of migrant life result in a remarkable translation of the metropolis itself – London is renamed Ellewondeeon in the invention of a 'foreign' tongue, and Rushdie tropicalises the weather. Suddenly the intimate lives and concerns of London's migrants and minorities emerge as major metropolitan themes and, in this translated terrain, they become agents of a historic transformation. You will remember the carnivalesque spirit of that scene in *The Satanic Verses*, when poetic justice is finally meted out: Mrs Torture is mercilessly taunted and eventually torched in a nightclub act where disco turns into *danse macabre*. Those who are excluded return to claim a place for themselves, to seize an alien time and make it their own and yours.

Literature, however, is often braver with the truth than life allows. The last decade is too close to me, too significantly a part of what is as yet in process, unfinished, for me to give it shape in this narrative. What I have learnt, so far, is this:

No name is yours until you speak it; somebody returns your call and suddenly, the circuit of signs, gestures, gesticulations, is established. You are part of a dialogue that may not be heard or heralded at first, but your person cannot be denied. The voices of the crossing, once drawn by the siren's song, may lead you astray, but strangely you find yourself the long way around. In another's country that is also your own, your person divides, and in following the forked path, you encounter yourself in a double movement . . . once as stranger, and then as friend.

James Berry

••••••••••••••••

Ancestors I Carry

James Berry is a pioneering voice in Black British writing. Drawing up on his African Jamaican roots, his best poetry is a dialogue with history. Angry at times, but never without compassion, he asks probing questions of both Africa and Europe. His anthology of Black British poetry, *News for Babylon*, was a ground-breaking achievement which showcased several new Black British poets in the 1980s. Now in his seventies, he is a celebrated poet with numerous prestigious prizes to his name. He continues to read his works in public.

In 1924, eighty-six years after the abolition of slavery, I was born in Boston, a rural and coastal village of Portland, in north-east Jamaica. The fourth of six children, I was soon brought home to Fair Prospect, three miles along the coast from Boston. Here, domed with regular orange blooms, around the hills and flatlands, above the common features of coconut palm trees, the mightily spreading poinciana, or flame tree, flourished in the drumming wash of the seasound. At a distance, the high trees hid vegetable gardens and tethered or penned domestic animals.

My parents had background histories in the two nearby former slave plantations of that area – Boston and Fair Prospect. With no wage earner in the family, we depended on sales from foodcrops we grew and domestic animals we reared. This meant that we children helped with the work to be done; it also meant that my mother, with my sister, her first child, made most of our clothes on her ancient Singer sewing machine. My father had built our house on his own land and had acquired other pieces of land that he worked. He would come home in the evening with melted sweets and overripe fruits squashed in his hot pockets for the youngest among us. He would get up nights and calmly help to nurse any sick one of us, just as he had an amazing skill to get sick animals better. Yet, I gradually began to develop quite an angry feeling against my father. I did not fully see it straight why this was so. Perhaps nobody saw or understood my feelings. My particular problems were probably simply not noticed; so nobody talked about them. Looking back now, I think I wanted my father to show me he could explore me and reveal my dissatisfactions to me. This was not going to happen.

My 1930s school days began at home with my share of feeding pigs and chickens, putting goats out to feed, fetching water, fetching the mule, the donkey. A quick bite of breakfast, a brisk wash, and away I went running, sweating, two miles away to Rural Hill School, my Church of England elementary school, where the church my family attended stood nearby. Being late, and getting locked out from morning hymn and prayers, usually meant lashes with the cane.

Our school was one enormous room like a big barn. The Head sat at his or her desk on the platform at one end. Floggings went on anywhere or at any time during the Babel of different and vocal classes in session together. Occasionally, sudden interest in a dramatic flogging would halt every class to immediate stillness and silence. This might be the kind of day when a big boy took on our headmaster, returning blows between his lashes to develop a tussling brawl of a fight. The whole school would instantly become hushed and enthralled by the horror, watching. It would take the firm shouting of a teacher to restore individual class business.

Not surprisingly, it could look as if we were at school to be subdued, mostly. Only an occasional boy or girl was able to show off carrying a whole textbook. As we got older – and stopped carrying a slate, or a piece of it – most boys carried their remnant piece of a book shoved in their pockets. We had no school library or any library service; there was never any common presence of books about. Where there was a textbook in a family, sharing it went through the home and was passed on to other child relatives. This meant that a textbook which had not lost its covers and some pages well into its middle would be a very new book indeed. In our own house the only whole books I can remember were the Bible, the hymn-book and our prayer book.

It was emphasised at school that our way of life was 'agricultural'. And, true, we had a school garden, and were sent into it once a week, but usually without a teacher or any instruction. We were also supposed to have a woodwork workshop which never materialised at all. There were other subjects, too, that never appeared.

Nothing else got everybody running about as excitedly as Empire Day celebrations on 24 May every year. While nothing existed that was called 'an African' or 'a Caribbean' poem, there were English poems we had to memorise, like *Try Again* by Eliza Cook, about King Bruce of Scotland and the spider. Anything worthwhile, impressive or memorable, emerged shining with a White face. By the time you got to the 'sixth class' you were well settled with your 'Memory Gem' – a piece of poetry you were given the chance to select as a personal choice that you wished to memorise and use as guidance to build your character. Mine was:

I will not waste my spring of youth
in idle dalliance
but will plant rich seeds
to blossom in my manhood
and bear fruit when I am old.

The teaching was full of arrivals of governors and visits of generals, sirs, lords, earls, dukes, ladies, colonels, majors, royal persons and the culture of the British Isles. A boy would be reprimanded or caned if a teacher caught him singing a Caribbean calypso. The acceptable would have been the singing of a song like *Drink to Me Only with thine Eyes* based on Ben Jonson's poem, or to be heard memorising a poem like *The Wreck of the Hesperus*. In word and deed, England was taught to be the Mother Country. And there was nothing in an elementary school lesson that ordinarily introduced a story in which a Black person was hero or heroine.

Lessons about Africa were usually about locating British Africa on the map, and studying what those places produced. Most children left school with a deep shame and hatred of Africa. One particularly embarrassing reading lesson that stayed vivid in the memory was an extract from Harriet Beecher Stowe's *Uncle Tom's Cabin* about a man in America, St Clare, who had mischievously bought a dirty, ugly and really odd nine year old slave girl, Topsy, and given her to his cousin, Miss Ophelia. Topsy was 'one of the Blackest of her race; and her round shining eyes . . . moved with quick and restless glances . . .'. St Clare told his cousin that he had bought Topsy for Miss Ophelia to educate her.

Astonished, fixed with disbelief, Miss Ophelia eventually sat down and asked, 'How old are you, Topsy?'

'Dun no, Missis', said the image, with a grin that showed all her teeth.

'Don't know how old you are? . . . Who was your mother?'

'Never had none!' said the child, with another grin.

'Never had any mother? . . . Where were you born?'

'Never was born!'

' . . . Do you know who made you?'

'Nobody as I knows on . . . I spect I grow'd. Don't think anybody never made me . . .'

We never studied Black characters. Why had this one popped up? To reflect our all-failure image? We found the extract both a worry and a puzzle, not quite seeing its relevance to ourselves, yet somehow feeling mocked and ridiculed, while never having any way of expressing that. So we merely kept that as one more of our Black-child's uncomfortable embarrassments and mysteries.

Topsy's ignorance of her own history and origins was mirrored in our own West Indian curriculum, which gave us no clearer sense of where we had come from, who we really were, how we contributed to the New World experience, and what our fair and free participation and development could be.

Another amazing part of our African-Jamaican school children's experience up to the 1940s was how schoolteaching drilled it into us that England was our Mother Country. Understanding practically nothing about the reality of slavery, its human-made hellfire and the traumas that we arrived from, we merely accepted that nobody talked about slavery. Teachers skipped across the subject. And neither grandparents nor parents talked about it. Nobody readily entered that soul-searing shame of their six to seven earlier generations. But children well understood that, like themselves, nobody liked Africans. And managing without lost mother-tongue languages, African names, customs and religious rituals – and not ever seeing a native African, even as a visitor – children never questioned the idea of mother-country England. In fact it offered a relief that, after all, one did have an acceptable motherland.

I left school at fifteen years old and came face to face with my insurmountable problem – my future. This was the year 1939 and war had broken out in Europe. I had brooded over my possible advanced education, my development and future, by far more seriously than my parents showed they understood. And this brooding was not straightforward: I was disappointed with myself.

I felt I had not fulfilled the promise, joy and excitement I had stirred in everyone for being able to read before I was four years old. I had been the celebrated child at home and in our village kindergarten. I could easily remember I had a happy side to my nature. I loved my mother's warm and selfless personality that went with her choir-singing voice around her six children. My four brothers were a joy. Not having any toys bought for us, we made our own bats and balls, wheels and pushcarts, kites and tops. We searched the woods for birds' nests and wild fruits. We fished from high rocks at the seaside and searched the beaches for smooth and round stones to use as marbles. With my auntie's sons we had enough participants to play cricket and other games. Apart from our houseland, we had a separate piece of lowland and two pieces of mountainland. But, I had long asked to be allowed to have extra studies with our head-master after school daily. As was customary, that work prepared students for local exams that could take them into advanced education. Yet, 'where was the money to come from? Eh?' my father had said. I was left broody, solemn, sad.

While my father could spend the best part of a day with a sick animal, he never read even a newspaper. I had long decided I would not speak only the way my father spoke, with his local village voice: he had got nowhere and was going nowhere. I took to speaking the way our school headmaster spoke, even when I was at home. More and more a strong feeling in me wanted to reject my father's personality. My father was happy – too happy – being totally static! And I began to notice too how critically angry my mother was, every time she found out he had gone and worked for the slave owner's descendant – the White woman at the old Great House – looking after her horses for nothing! Repeating how the lady actually asked my father to come and work for nothing – nothing – my mother spat out her bitterest rage. But, nobody knew how deeply depressed I was myself. Nobody knew I tried secretly to write poetry that came with a biblical tone or that I well knew it was neither fit to show nor read aloud to anybody.

Whether hearing them read aloud or reading them myself, both the Psalms and some Old Testament stories had provided my really first impact of literature. Immediately I had under-stood how Abraham offered his son Isaac to God as sacrifice and how God said he would provide his own lamb, emotion clogged my throat and tears washed my face. Less overwhelming, a strange, outer, sensation affected me most times when I was alone in the fields looking after our animals or doing work given me. I got used to it and would sit down or simply stand and feel and examine the sensation like a dreaded mystery aroused around me, which I took to be the spirit of trees. Perhaps my own mystery challenged me, I did not know how. I had dismissed my father's life as that of a free slave and knew I was right, but could not even begin to imagine any acceptable future ahead in which I would express myself.

Withdrawn, solemn, feeling like a shadow, I took up the shoemaker's apprenticeship my parents negotiated for me. I was no good at that. I took up the tailor's apprenticeship they fixed up: I was not good at that either. I simply stopped going. Soon I saw 'Agents Wanted' in the newspapers and wrote a letter off immediately. Taken on to sell insurance, patent medicines and beauty products, I sold my own animals and bought an old bicycle. Anything that would keep me from a donkey back, with bag and machete – anything that would suggest a non-villager's occupation – would be great.

Bicycling about with my suitcase of goods – getting to know the people and homes of distant and surrounding districts – I gradually found an unexpected joy: the self-challenging occupation became self-expanding in the most incalculable ways. Then also, feeling inquisitive about the lady of the old Great House and her way of life, I accepted her offer to come and do a waiting job for her at occasional dinner or lawn parties, where she entertained society people and even film stars. Then, nearly four years after leaving school I came face to face with that single opportunity I needed to get away from Fair Prospect.

Like a hurricane, news came racing through the village that Americans had fixed up business with Jamaica and Britain for Jamaicans to be recruited to do seasonal work on American farms. The war had drained away their usual source of farmworkers.

I and my friend Lenny met up with excited anticipation. There were a limited number of places allocated to different areas. Getting a place depended on the District Constable's critical judgement of character, health, age and even need. We hurried to the DC's house. Joking us, he gave us both a card instantly. Getting a travel visa still depended on passing a medical examination by American doctors. Weight requirements asked for a minimum of 140 lbs. I was apprehensive about that, with good reason. Lenny and I were both eighteen years old but he was much stouter and instantly passed his test, while my weight of 110 lbs caused the doctors to confer before agreeing that I was perfectly fit, healthy and OK. Yet such an important change was hardly going to happen in our world without our coming face to face with a new kind of unexpected shock, embarrassment or sheer act of degradation.

The reality was that our African, British and Jamaican history had taken us through a hell-hole of fire called slavery and left us with that historical experience and its scars unexplained. And the official line, as well as school lessons and folk knowledge, all colluded with the withholding of information. One could only assume that the pain, the horror, the shame of this experience were all too much. I had myself made one or two amazing discoveries, by chance.

Living between schooldays and adulthood, idle, troubled, feeling lost, wandering about, I had been struck suddenly by the fact that the land our house was built on was called 'Negro House'. I saw too that the site was just about three to four minutes' brisk walk from the old plantation sugarmill, its works-yard and its nearby overseer's, bookkeeper's and servants' quarters, with the shining Plantation House a little distance away. Surely, our home stood on a site where slave-quarters had stood in row after row. And hence the name – 'Negro House'. I remembered, when we had dug up the land, making our vege-table garden, we were amazed by the bits of clay pots and bowls we had found. Then, I remembered, as children we played on the ruins of the old plantation sugarmill. And we had no idea whatsoever that the crumbling pillars, the roofless walls, the rusty iron ruins, were all the skeleton bits of the old slavery sugarmill. I had remembered how, with its little distance, the tower of the old windmill practically overlooked our house. Then, halfway through schooldays, though never mentioned, never discussed, that word 'Negro' had always stood out like a dagger for me. Whenever it cropped up, obviously written by a White writer, it began to come at me like a held instrument expressing a sadistic antithesis of what a real human being was assumed to be.

Having passed our medical now, we walked away happily starry-eyed, talking about our most prized 'Yankee Passport'. But, as I examined the new identity card an intense chill shot through me and held me to sudden silence. I asked Lenny if he noticed that in the space provided for 'race', our identity was stamped in as 'Negro'. Lenny looked and expressed surprise. I told him I was Jamaican and never saw myself as any 'Negro'. He agreed. What sort of a person did he see as Negro, I asked him. Lenny burst out laughing, saying 'absolutely the worst person in the world'. Even when Lenny laughed inappropriately he had a way of getting you to laugh with him, but I didn't laugh this time. I pointed out how 'Negro' simply meant 'Black' and nation identities were not based on skin colour. Europeans were not called 'blancos' or 'snows' or 'chalks' or anything like that. I didn't have books to read or anybody to discuss these matters with, but my gut feeling told me that the stuck identity of 'Negro' was false and wrong and stayed stuck for vile racial reasons.

On a brilliant June day in 1943, an American troopship sailed from Jamaica with some three hundred of us, all men, to New Orleans, USA. In a military camp, with general amenities provided, plus five dollars a week and camp entertainment, while we waited to be transported to an allocated farm, I experienced the most exhilarating three-week holiday of my life. I shared camp with men of varied backgrounds from all round Jamaica. And we had time: time to talk, tell stories, play musical instruments and sing, play games, meet my Jamaica in its different layers as I had never known it. Leaving here, I was to work on farms in Minnesota, New York State, Iowa, Florida, Connecticut and New Jersey.

Whatever the mixture of qualities that America had, it was all to be mightily stimulating. Farmers welcomed us like a rescuing party. They liked how as West Indians we were different. One farmer said, 'You boys are *sure* different from our own Negroes. You talk with such *fine* Oxford accent.' But I was going to be shocked, outraged and deeply saddened by the way the nation had instituted a race prejudice culture against its Black citizens. As for us, we would see we were similarly placed. One example: I and my friend were thrown off a bus on a country road in Florida. He had sat in a seat reserved for Whites. Though he declared he was '*British*', the White driver pulled his gun on us, saying: 'Niggers are jes niggers.' To see a Black person's picture in the newspapers was usually to see a Black man handcuffed beside a White policeman, or being there accompanying a crime report. Yet, there were more opportunities in America for me beyond anything I had known; and I had regular earnings.

All kinds of homestudy courses were advertised in the newspapers. I didn't know exactly why I took up mechanical dentistry. I moved to work on a different farm frequently. Yet, truly, packages of the correspondence course followed me. And the skill I learnt was really going to be helpful later. In 1947 – after four years – I returned home to my Jamaican village.

My two younger brothers had become beautiful young men. My mother still practised her choir-singing at home. My father still shaved only once a week. With our village band, which included two old schoolmates, my brothers organised a homecoming all-night moonlight party in our yard, which would live in my memory throughout the rest of my life.

I told my home people that the USA had been my university. I played down how as a Black person in America I had learned how to carefully approach the White and beautiful people as I would a wild beast. I did not tell them how Black people, who for some two hundred years had worked without pay, building the nation, watched new White settlers from all round the world come and reap benefits of America's educational and other institutions that they were denied. I did not tell them if I knew what I know now I could not have been the self of my good Sunday school boy, seeing how the churches sat back and watched the active brutalisation of Black people. I had come home with more money than all my family had, put together. And, soon, like water sprinkled on hot desert ground, my savings would vanish. But, luckily, after a year at home, by happy chance, another panic to get away happened.

The British troop-ship *Empire Windrush* had dropped off returning servicemen and advertised for passengers on its homebound run to England at twenty-eight pounds and ten shillings per passage. Nobody had heard of any such offer before and there was a rush to book up. My friend Lenny caught the *Windrush* to England; I caught the *SS Orbita* three months later. I disembarked at Liverpool in September 1948, knowing that Lenny was still accommodated temporarily in the Clapham air-raid shelter. Employment officers advised us that work was available in Oxford; I went there – £15 in my pocket.

Eventful happenings resulting from my going to Oxford were: on my first day at work, at a government ordinance depot, I discovered I was partnered up to work with an Englishman namesake, James Berry, of similar age as myself; at the weekend I met a West Indian Oxford University student who invited me to tea at his lodgings with his friends; I came to understand that the hostel I stayed in was near to the home of the woman I would meet six years later in London and marry. But, after a few weeks, I felt Oxford had turned out not to be my true destination. At twenty-three years old I needed London.

I arrived at Victoria Station in early November in misty chilly weather of early night. With no address to go to, I approached three policemen separately, before I found a place with a vacancy: a Rowton House. They had rooms at two shillings and sixpence a night. Relieved, I booked in for four nights.

The room was sparse and cold, with only one army blanket on the bed. Next morning the place amazed me. I came downstairs and the place stank of unwashed bodies mixed with the smells of kippers being grilled and sausages fried. I came closer and saw an incredible group of people – some with sores bandaged, others with sticks and crutches, others dirty and beggar-dressed – having breakfast, making it in a vast open room with ranges of hot-surface cookers, or simply sitting about. The shocking people looked like the flocked grouping of the city's down-and-outs. Saying to myself, 'Surely, this is not the London I have come to,' I nippily tripped out, collected back my seven shillings and sixpence down-payment for three more nights, collected my suitcase from the left-luggage place and started walking, looking for any room-to-let adverts.

I had a little breakfast somewhere. Then, carrying my suitcase I walked on, looking at adverts for rooms to let, then walked on again, taken up with the bomb-gutted buildings of London. I took a tramcar a second time; when it stopped I saw a long queue of mostly Black men. I hurried off the tramcar with my luggage and approached the queue.

The men bantered me, asking if I was a 'jus'-come'. This was the Labour Exchange, Brixton, they said. Did I have an address? No. Well – if I wanted to join the queue to sign on for work, I needed an address first. To get a room I should go across the road, over to Somerleyton Road, number so-and-so, and see the tall and lanky Jamaican – married to a White woman – Mr Gus Leslie.

The property owner, Mr Leslie, placed me sharing a room with a fellow-Jamaican I had met on the ship. My half of the rent would be one pound and fifteen shillings a week, here at 37 Somerleyton Road, Brixton. The room offered me a single bed, two blankets and shared use of a gasring on the floor to make meals on. It was a terrific relief to find a place to stop; though, surely, I would not stay here long. I collected my ration book and things continued to go well.

I went into a nearby grocery shop to do my shopping and

stood. Strangely, I felt someone I didn't see looking at me. I turned round and instantly thought: what a way this blue-eyed, black-haired English woman reminded me of my mother! She came and served me my purchases. At the end, she picked up an unrationed half-pound of sugar and said, 'This is extra sugar for you. It comes from your own country anyway.' And she gave me that extra sugar every time I went in and did my shopping.

London elated me. I went about looking, feeling an extra-ordinary new sense of freedom. London's voices didn't scare me as New York's voices did. Not only familiar, these voices were friendlier. People had time to stop and assist with a direction. And, now, here was Big Ben! Now – here was the great waterway Teacher had gone on about, 'London is built on the River Thames!' Now – here was Trafalgar Square. The pigeons! The heavenward statue of Lord Horatio Nelson! And here now, man, here now was Buckingham Palace . . .! How could circumstances have kept this magic world of London away from a young country fellow's eyes? Then – then – there was that real hope of regular money. MONEY, man, MONEY! Soon, though, tireless failed attempts to find a job and different accommodation made me feel my good luck had all evaporated.

At last, it looked very likely I would get taken on at a biscuit factory just outside London. I arrived at the factory. The keeper at the porter's lodge wouldn't let me in. While I pleaded with him, the manager appeared and told him to let me in.

A gent of an Englishman, the manager offered me a comfortable chair in his office. He then held a fine-smelling box of cigars for me to take one. Undaunted by my polite refusal – to now suggest he had an ongoing policy about West Indians – he became profusely apologetic about how he dared not take me on, well knowing all his staff would instantly walk out. I stood up swiftly, telling him many thanks for bothering. Then, going through the Wanted Ads in the newspaper, I actually saw three advertisements asking for dental mechanics' assistants.

This was 1948: year of the new National Health scheme.

People were tumbling over each other for new dentures. Hadn't I brought along a little pile of lessons of my American correspondence course?

All evening I refreshed my memory with theoretical skills on dental mechanics and wrote my job application letter. I received a reply by return of post, was given an interview, and within a few days I was a dental mechanic's assistant, working in a little room at the back of a surgery on Kennington Road. Too shut away for me, too uninspiring, this work bored me. After nearly three years, I left and took up the training to become an International Telegraphist with Post Office Cable and Wireless in 1951.

Now here was a job for me. Outside Temple Station, beside the Thames, Electra House would engage me with its buzz on four floors round the clock for twenty-six years. Till more people came from the West Indies and India – and I had the chance to meet other islanders from the British Caribbean – our staff came mostly from round the UK. I would enjoy working here. At my bedsit, I worked on correspondence courses in English and Journalism. I would come more and more into the joy of libraries and their books and writing workshops and theatre-going. I would develop my short story and poetry writing. This was going to be my pattern of life for many years ahead. My severest difficulty had been that I had not been able to change my gasring-on-the-floor accommodation at Somerleyton Road.

Much of my spare time then went into trying to find new accommodation. I would meet little clusters of fellow West Indians at accommodation notice boards. All of us would be astounded by open rejections that stated: *No Blacks. No Coloureds. No Irish. No dogs.* Then, one Saturday morning, answering an ad, I went to 13 Effra Road, Brixton. The landlady opened the door and let me in. I felt, surely, this must be a dream. The London-Russian Jewish woman actually showed me a large room, with shared kitchen and bath, and then and there offered me the accommodation – without reference. After I lived here for two years, a Jamaican boxer friend, Lloyd Barnett, passed on his Maida Vale flat to me.

Dance halls and clubs were refusing entry to West Indians. Managers had introduced a pretext that a quota system was being applied to us, which really meant we were told at the door that our quota was full or only one or two more could be allowed in. Lloyd Barnett, myself and others organised what we called the West Indian Dance Club. By this we built up a list of members and notified them of our monthly dances at prominent halls around London. With a popular band, like Johnny Dankworth, and added attractions like calypso singers and feature dancers, the events were popular. As secretary, I know we did not make profits to keep, but we contributed to a social need. Also, I became secretary to the Caribbean and African Social and Cultural Club, in the Paddington area. That did not exist trouble-free. We had to report to the police that a nearby publican refused us service and harassed us, declaring that long-standing customers objected to the presence of Blacks in their local pub. Then it became obvious that the police were turning a blind eye when local White youths waylaid members of our club and beat them up. When our members retaliated and became the ones arrested and the real facts came out in court, entrance to the club's premises became piled and blocked with lavatory excreta, with a thorough daubing of the club door. At our meeting, everybody was angry, sad, hurt. Yet it seemed a thoughtful feeling or two came out.

Somebody talked about how human beings were wild and frightened till tamed. Which lookalike flock didn't prefer their own group company only, till tamed? Didn't human beings need to be introduced to a new relationship? As West Indians we had the Mother Country England schooled and drilled into us. Had Mother England introduced us, the outside brothers and sisters? The British institutions reflected no such multiracial element. Neither had the number one symbol of Empire and 'Mother Country' unity, Buckingham Palace, showed any Black face on its staff or anywhere connected.

Owner, Millard Johnson, lived on the club's premises. He saw to it that talks, discussions, play sketches, the occasional specially featured and hosted personality – like Chief Minister of Jamaica, Sir Norman Manley and the Kabaka of Buganda – and the purely social events, were all still carried on. I stayed on the club's committee, even though the burden of the general cost of living made me change address.

I gave up my Maida Vale flat and moved to a shared bedsitter, with an actor friend, on Westbourne Street, Paddington. We felt at home there for a few months – till two weeks before Christmas – when we were given notice to leave. Shocked, panic-stricken, we rushed to see the housekeeper. There was nothing they could do, she protested. They had forgotten the clause in their contract forbidding tenancy to a Black person. A letter from the house-owner's solicitors had threatened them. I most luckily found a room in West Hampstead.

Beginning to know people from other British Caribbean islands seemed to arouse another dimension of myself. Through attending talks and socials at the West Indian Student Centre, Earls Court, I began to share literary interests with them. I came to know the best-known literary magazine, *Bim*, based in Barbados and edited by the famous Frank Collymore. And before too long I would start contributing short stories to *Bim* myself. A Trinidadian in my telegraph office invited me to a party. Here, I met my future wife, Mary, a social worker, whose Oxford home stood only a short distance from the hostel where I stayed for my first six weeks in England.

Mary was well into the arts generally, but poetry particularly. She was a member of a poetry writers' group in Golders Green, headed by artist and sound poet Bob Cobbing. My first date with her was her invitation to her writers' group when they studied T. S. Eliot's *The Wasteland*. I had heard the name *Eliot*, but had read absolutely nothing of his. In fact, this was 1956: I was steeped in developing short story writing and interests that went with that.

As I sat absorbed by the reading, the music of Eliot's words became a spell, wooing my awareness to a more and more uplifted sympathy to a kind of fresher and fresher wordless knowing. Perhaps I was so moved and held so strangely spellbound that at the end I did not want to speak, and explained nothing. A week later, while cleaning my room, I felt an extraordinary rhythmic spell of a sound in my head, till I suddenly knew the words and wrote them down. I saw I had a short, significant but unimpressive poem, in Jamaican Creole language. Here is that first poem:

I de one they call Simple Joe.
They talk, they laugh, they vex 'bout me.
But days gone, like days a-acome, do walk
with new talk, new laugh, new vexation, nah!

Dramatic as all that was, I did not really begin writing poetry till three to four years afterwards.

My short stories and sketches were to find first outlets through George Scott, editor of the literary monthly publication, *Truth*. Through that exposure, a BBC radio producer tried me out and then had me broadcast stories I submitted. Following that, I broadcast short occasional radio scripts for editor Wyn Knowles, on *Woman's Hour*, over quite a period. Then I found myself drawn into intense poetry writing workshops.

On to the mid sixties and well up into the seventies, I saw my poetry writing development work settled in two most influential workshops in London: a City Literary Institute workshop tutored by Geoffrey Adkins with the gifted member Ted Burford, and Poets' Workshop at the Poetry Society, Earls Court, tutored by Irving Weinman, and including famous-to-be members like George Macbeth, Judith Kazantzis, James Sutherland Smith and Laurie Smith. And it is most notable that it was through Limestone Publications magazine, at the City Lit, edited by Geoffrey Adkins, that I had the first edition of *Bluefoot Traveller* – that first anthology of 11 UK Caribbean poets – published in 1976.

My association with the Caribbean Artists Movement's activities, as an assistant programme organiser, based at the New Beacon Bookshop in London, brought me into contact with its proprietor John La Rose, the historian Kamau Braithwaite, writer Andrew Salkey and a host of Caribbean creative artists. My own first selection of poems, *Fractured Circles*, was brought out by John La Rose and Sarah White's publishing outfit. Through Chatto and Windus's editor Andrew Motion, there was a significant increase in the exposure of UK Caribbean poets' voices in my anthology, *News for Babylon*. Outstanding new talents like Grace Nichols, John Agard, Linton Kwesi Johnson and Frederick d'Aguiar were anthologised with already known poets like Andrew Salkey and E. A. Markham.

In 1977 my telegraphist job blessed me with early retirement. Now there was nothing else but writing. Making up stories, poems, plays. Using up all those notes I had crammed into notebooks about ideas, characters, overheard bits of dialogue. I wanted now to be answerable to nothing and nobody but myself. For some time I was a voluntary member of the Arts Council Community Arts Panel, helping to assess the funding needs of community-based arts groups. Then I found myself answering an advert for a C. Day Lewis Fellowship at a Lambeth comprehensive school. I was awarded the residency. The two thousand pounds was most useful, as I had used up my early retirement lump sum to clear my house mortgage.

This new back-to-school experience opened my eyes. The reality was that the school library shelves served the Black children poorly. Their nearest cultural reading material came from the American-based perspective of the writer Rosa Guy and one book by the London-based Indian writer Farouk Dhondy. The few copies of the thin biography of a local Black girl, locally published, were not only always out but dog-eared with pages missing when sighted. I helped the librarian to find new material but with little satisfactory success. The residency had me turning my thoughts to writing for children. With great luck my first book of stories, *A Thief in the Village*, won the Smarties Award for Children's books; and my next, a book of

poems for children, *When I Dance*, received the Signal Poetry
Award. In between those two, I had also been declared winner
of the National Poetry Prize, 1981, for my adult poem, *Fantasy of
an African Boy*. I was shocked when in 1990 I was called for an
OBE and tremendously elated when in 1991 I was nominated
for a Cholmondeley Award for Poets.

Among my most moving experiences in England was to
witness Black Study adult students at work in groups in London
in the 1970s. Recognising many of the participants as people
from rural districts similar to the one I came from, and seeing
them in discussions about Egypt and Africa generally, seeing
their faces and hearing their comments and responses – con-
sidering, particularly, that since school many here would not
have opened a book – I knew an important change had happened. The experience inspired the poem, 'Black Study
Students', published in *Fractured Circles* in 1979. I was moved
to similar feelings at the Black Writers workshops in Brixton. I
became most elated and thoughtful too on visiting Jamaica and
discovered that three of my last year classmate pupils at school
had become professionals by their academic achievements.
Charles Panton had become a scientist in America; Lucy Panton
had become a working doctor in an American hospital; Olga
Scott had become an established and well-respected head-
teacher, there in Jamaica.

It turned out that, later, in the 1980s, I and Buchi Emecheta
were invited to conduct the first Black Writers' Workshop at the
Writers Centre, Arvon at Lumb Bank.

Farrukh Dhondy

✦✦✦✦✦✦✦✦✦✦✦✦✦✦✦✦✦✦✦✦✦✦✦

Speaking in Tongues

Farrukh Dhondy's fiction sprang out of a very particular era in the
radical politics of race.

His collections of stories opened out the largely unseen worlds
of young people in London's East End – particularly Black and
Asian – caught in the double binds of race, discrimination and
poverty as well as of community conservatism and resistance to
change. Dhondy's strengths are those of a born communicator and
interpreter. (It is fitting that he worked for a number of years
subsequently as a Commissioning Editor for Channel 4.) Their sharp
observational quality and utter lack of patronisation make them
a good monument to a time that began to give voice to very
different survivors of a different sort of crossing.

When I was sixteen I left my home town of Poona and
went to Bombay, the big city, to do a course in Chemical
Engineering at the University. I was bewildered and lonely in
Bombay and I hated Chemical Engineering and every wretched
equation connected with its study.

I lived in the flat of a grand-uncle of mine, a great and
generous man who was a staunch Gandhian and would only
wear clothes of homespun cotton and eat a strict vegetarian diet.
These were the early sixties, the Gandhian agenda was at an
end and my grand-uncle's experiments with truth had been
boiled down to prayer, to astounding and sometimes disgusting

feats of yoga and to the personal distribution of hundreds of umbrellas to the poor during the monsoons.

All of it, including the lectures in thermodynamics and changing suburban trains in the Bombay rush hour, drove me mad. Yet I knew that I had contrived to deserve all of it, a punishment for the twin sins of literalness and vanity.

It was the practice amongst all those who passed their 'Intermediate' year of a science college, throughout the length and breadth of India, to apply either to medical institutes or one or other college of technology. My mark at the exam had been good, even exceptional – no great feat of the intellect in any objective terms, but singular enough to get me a coveted place on the most coveted course. I had to apply and I had to accept the place when it was offered, if only so that I could spend the next few months, out of short-sighted vanity, impressing my class-mates and teachers with the fact.

The sin of literalness was inherent in the residue of Indian nationalism from which we all suffered, from resonating slogans about being useful to the country, building the nation and finding a career in a field which would in the near future demand irrigation with talent – well-paid talent. The literal bent of mind made me and my advisers, teachers, friends and most of all my family elders, look no further than the expansion of Indian industry, medicine, economics and law.

After a few months of being on the Chemical course, I gave up the struggle with the vengeful Bombay monsoon and with suburban trains. I discovered a tram that ran the length of Bombay from where I lived to the doorstep of the college. It took a couple of hours each way, but it afforded me seating space for the whole journey and every morning I would set out on it with paperbacks I had bought from the pavement bookshops.

I read Lawrence Durrell's Alexandria Quartet end to end, four books with a secret interconnection of a time-space continuum which only I of all the tram-travellers could understand! Here was a richness of language, contrived, self-conscious, sentimentally exaggerated, that precisely answered the needs of my loneliness, my Bombay blues.

Here was a story about people who lived in Egypt and weren't all white. People who were taken as seriously as the satirised British caricatures or the Bohemian British philosopher-hero. If Arabs could be written into the narrative web of what I prematurely thought was a masterpiece, then so could Indians. I wanted to be a writer. No more Chemical Engineering. Here was a brighter conceit.

I left Bombay and went to Delhi, telling my parents that I had renounced all career ambitions, braving their grave and desperate disapproval and, again from the pavement bookstalls, I began the reading that privately promised me membership of the club of aspiring writers. Reading Durrell's letters, essays and travelogues took me to Henry Miller and to D. H. Lawrence, to Cavafy and Kazantzakis in translation. A lot of it was a waste of time, none of it was evaluated in any deep sense and I didn't know anyone with whom I could discuss what I was voraciously reading. Durrell seemed to have formed, with Miller and the memory of Lawrence (someone whom neither Miller nor Durrell had ever met), a small, charmed, special, knowing, literary sect. God, I wanted to be part of that sect!

There was no way in. I was back in Poona and wanting to get out of India. The real test of vanity would be to apply to the big universities, and for several snobbish and historical reasons there seemed to be only two that fitted this bill, Oxford or Cambridge, and that's what I did.

Growing up in India in those years meant listening to and taking part in two debates about writing, one public, one internal. The public debate was not a widespread preoccupation of the general populace. Within this populace, in the two or three decades after Independence from colonial rule, there was a debate about which language would be used in official trans-actions and which languages would be the medium in schools and universities. The debate had a literary adjunct. Should Indian writers write in English at all?

To admit that one thought in English was somehow to admit that one's mind still wore the uniform of the departed conqueror.

There had been a handful of Indian writers in English, both in fiction and non-fiction, but to use English at all was seen by some to be a betrayal of the Indian consciousness and since one didn't possess any other, a betrayal of the material of one's experience.

I can't quite say how or why this debate fizzled out, but it's certainly true that those writers and poets whose first or best language happened to be English, because it was the language of their disciplined reading and of their critical awareness, began to assert the right of English to be recognised as Indian, shoulder to shoulder with Urdu, Hindi, Bengali or Gujerati. India emerged from its blinding nationalism as its intellectual and economic commerce with the world grew, using English as the language of communication. That was the start and finish of the open debate.

The internal debate was a very old one which, crudely stated, proposed the substitution of Odes to Nightingales with Odes to Bulbuls and addresses to roses which are sick, with addresses to lotuses or jasmine buds similarly afflicted. It was a canker of a debate and gave rise to silly self-questioning – where the relationship between people called Wooster and Jeeves could be funny, could there be an Indian equivalent? The answer is, of course, yes, there could be a hundred interesting, even hilarious formats exploring the relationship between particular classes of Indians in an ironic servant-master relationship. The trick was to find the pattern in the carpet, the story in day to day goings on.

Two literary events settled the internal debate in the years in which I was plotting my exit, working at my exams in order to win a scholarship and get a place at one of the 'chosen' Universities. I wasn't Jude the Obscure but I did understand how he felt.

The first intervention was that of a novelist called John Wain who was booked to speak at the Poona Philosophical Society, a sleepy gathering of academics who met once a fortnight to discuss Bertrand Russell's contentions on God or unravel the connections between Vedanta and Atomic Physics in a narrow tutorial room of the gothic, black-stoned Ferguson College.

The John Wain lecture was heavily oversubscribed and had to be moved to a lecture theatre in the same place because very many citizens had turned up in the mistaken belief that Mr Wain was a famous cowboy. The crowd grew shifty when they didn't recognise their hero, but Mr Wain, probably amazed at the response to his coming, braved the crowds with an address on the state of the English novel with allusions to Kingsley Amis and Iris Murdoch which passed through the audience like gamma rays from a distant galaxy. Nevertheless they clapped, as much I thought, for the relief of its end as for the lecture itself.

A few weeks later a magazine called *Encounter*, which was widely read in India, carried an article by John Wain on his trip to Poona. He didn't mention the lecture but he made a story out of his visit to the little bungalow in the middle of our college where our Principal, the logician and philosopher Mr Damle, lived. Mr Wain described the house, the furnishings, the tea, the conversation and the small army of cockroaches which invaded the floor and his consciousness to the exclusion of everything else. The end of the essay was a lament for Indian education. I read it with fascination. It was an invitation to test reality against prose, because here it was, the Eng Lit essay by a published person about my own college in Poona. The descriptions were precise, recognisable. The jerky and finally pathetic personality of our college Principal was well captured and the pathos of his house and position as a 'logician' poignantly and even sympathetically sketched.

Of course it wasn't the whole story. John Wain would have had to stay longer to know how Professor Damle rose to prominence in the society of Brahmins who ran the college and awarded him his turn at the helm. There was more to the diminutive Damle than tea, tarnished Aristotelian logic and cockroaches.

But Wain had done me a service. He had seen that pattern in the carpet which had grown dusty with my footsteps. It was not only possible to write about Principal Damle, it was irreverent, precise in its own way and interesting.

The second comet to cross this gaze towards a literary horizon was V. S. Naipaul's book *An Area Of Darkness*. It was a beginning. It was a brown man, albeit from abroad, trying to see India without nationalistic spectacles, without guilt, almost without ideology. It was refreshing. Everyone who read English argued about it. It was in India bigger than Rushdie was later to be in Iran.

The book was condemned for being in the tradition of Katharine Mayo and Beverly Nichols who had written disparagingly of India in the thirties and forties, at the height of the nationalist movement against the British Raj. I knew that it was no such thing. It was a nail in the cross of blind nationalism, and this crucifixion felt necessary.

The book was not so much a travelogue but more of an imaginative excursion that no-one had dared to take. It was not a great formal invention – a trip across India with the travelogue in mind and a sharpness of perception that only a foreigner could bring to the subject. It was a book waiting to be written and this expatriate descendant of indentured Indian labour rushed in, with genius, where others feared to tread.

Despite these examples, I came to Cambridge University to study Physics, not English Literature. We called it 'reading Natural Sciences', but that was part of the appeal, speaking in tongues. There were ideas, fashions and conceits in the styles, conversations and in the very air of the place.

For me the strongest of these, the most ensnaring idea and the one that has stayed with me the longest was the conviction that one poem is demonstrably better than another and that the demonstration consists of a critical dialogue with the text in hand, calling upon the richness of experience that went into its construction.

The idea came from the work of F. R. Leavis and his associates and it mattered not whether you were reading History or Slavonic Studies, it had spread through the intellectual fabric of the place as fluoride spreads through water. Even those who were articulately against fluoridation drank it. The big idea spreads naturally to novels, to music, to philosophies, to religious experience and ultimately to values and ways of life. For a would-be writer, this powerful idea is a curse. It's an inhibition. Even though the newly learnt critical art makes it self-evident that D. H. Lawrence is a finer writer than Lawrence Durrell or Henry Miller, the analysis of writing makes it harder to do it. It was a common cry: the critical cramps the creative.

Or that was a way of dodging the truth which was that I was not convinced, not totally convinced that anyone would want to read any story I had to tell. My material hadn't found me.

When I had finished my studies in England there was no home in India to go back to. After a spell of depressing unemployment my father had found a job as an immigrant engineer in Iran. The rented house in the narrow lanes of a casbah in Isphahan was now 'home'. Or it was England and the challenge of writing something that someone would want to read? I chose London and took a job as a school teacher because a friend advised me to 'go to the Inner London Education Authority, they take anybody!'

Before I got employment as a teacher I drifted, doing odd jobs, washing dishes, painting houses, selling the occasional article to journalist agencies. The anonymity of this life was on the one hand exhilarating, a freedom from all bonds of social responsibility and a temptation to live in a totally 'existential' mode, imitating Jean Genet or characters in Camus for kicks, and on the other a condition of total powerlessness. It was not that I was kicked in the head every day by racist mobs, though it did happen once or twice, nor that white people spat on you in public, but more the fact that you didn't exist as a social entity in the fabric of Britain. You were nobody.

Politics is the pursuit of dignity. I signed up. I had been a member of a very close-knit Indian Workers' Association in the

Midlands and now I signed up to the secretive and serious cabal called the Black Panther Movement.

Despite being called a Movement, it hadn't thought very hard about where it was going. It spent a lot of time on 'discipline' which could mean anything from not being late for the six or seven weekly 'collective' meetings or initiating agitational activity in the Leninist mould – printing a paper, selling it at tube stations and street markets, waiting for the contradictions of racist bourgeois society to catch up with it. The group grew without direction even though there were clear tendencies emerging within it. Some of the members wanted to turn the young immigrant organisation, mostly Afro-Caribbean with a smattering of smart Asians, into a Baden-Powell troop, helping old ladies with their housing and shopping. Others wanted to turn to undeclared and sinister purposes bordering on imitation of the Irish Republican Army's robbing of banks, planting of bombs and arms practice. I belonged to the soft faction which started a literary group to read our poems to each other, canvassed for there to be a regular paper to be written and printed by ourselves and for 'organisational work' in the immigrant communities.

There were other groups of blacks with the same dilemmas at the time. It was a game with several serious consequences. People fought the police, they were tried for agitation, for conspiracy, for riot, for bodily harm, grievous and aggravated. Some went to jail, some went mad. The flat in which I lived was fire-bombed one dawn and I jumped from the second floor window, with any cover I could grab as I suffocated, onto the exploded glass on the pavement. Par for the course.

I began teaching in schools to earn some money and was immediately drawn to the challenge of it. The schools that would employ me had a vast number of black children and they didn't quite know what to do with them. I didn't know either but was determined to find out in my first few hours facing a class. To not do so would be to invite destruction. They were naughty children, bewildered in the main by the process of liberal schooling. They expected either a tight slap or they expected to get away with it and hone their skills of defiance against the will and prepared tasks of the teacher.

The 'Movement' published an amateur paper called *Freedom News*. In the interests of proletarianism, a few of us swallowed our literary education and pride and contributed whole-heartedly to what we knew in our heart of hearts was a poor cousin of Lenin's *Iskra* and a tatty version of the professional hippy newspapers of the sixties and early seventies. But there was nothing else. There was no other rag or bag which represented the voice of angry or posturing immigrants.

For *Freedom News* each week, or whenever it emerged, I wrote an anonymous 'story' about life in a tough multiracial London school. An editor working at a publishing house, a young white man with some sympathy for left-wing causes, used to buy the newspaper from the pavement sellers and read the pieces from the chalk zoo. He enterprisingly sought me out.

The 'comrades' who sold the newspapers were conspiratorially reluctant to relay to him the name of the author of the pieces. He may after all be a secret police agent or a member of the CIA.

Martin Pick, after an abortive foray into the wrong 'bad' school – he was guessing and chose the one with the naughtiest reputation – found me and offered me my first writing contract for a book of short stories.

Britain was ready for 'multicultural' writing before it existed.

The demand for it came with unbearably ponderous baggage. If young black and brown people could see themselves in stories it would build their confidence in their identity. It was deemed psychologically traumatic for the black and brown readers of Britain to not recognise themselves in books and turn page after page to imagine white men being heroic and white women being beautiful. These pseudo-political considerations are of course garbage, but into such a pool of expectation I cast my first stories. Macmillan published *East End At Your Feet* and the editors immediately began talking about a second book and a third.

There was no way that the money being offered for these stories, novels or memoirs would have kept me alive. I had to continue teaching, but there was no shortage of demand for such writing.

The Americans had fielded a genre of 'black' writing in the sixties, shifting the pendulum from James Baldwin's pensées to the radical, mother-fucking rhetoric of Eldridge Cleaver, Bobby Seale and George Jackson. These rebel writers, following Malcolm X, gave a white American readership the opportunity to expiate the discomfort and guilt of race in the USA by doing no more than buying a book and talking about it at dinner parties.

In Britain there was no race war. Some of the rhetoric and a few of the confidence tricks of such a war had crossed the Atlantic and a petty imitative game had started and petered out. A con man calling himself Michael X wrote his own autobiography full of fantasy and mendacious claims. As a 'writer' and revolutionary he had certainly found his material – bullying rhetoric which was the written equivalent for white readers of being whipped for a fee in Bayswater. He came to a sad end, running from himself and his discovered frauds to Trinidad where he murdered a few people, among them a British woman with aristocratic connections who had followed him there to live on his 'commune'. When the bodies of his victims were discovered he fled to Guyana and was captured deep in the savannah, defeated and played out. They hanged him and even as they did, his supporters in England appealed for mercy for this 'writer' and 'victim of racism'.

Finding a voice is inseparable from finding an audience. And yet once I had found a particular audience through four or five books whose stories came from the new ghettos, the frightened communities, I wanted to put a distance between the sympathy of this audience and myself. The sympathy had turned sour, become perverse. It was making its own demands and there were other writers expanding into the vacuum with autobiographical hard luck stories.

Winning sympathy for oneself through writing defeats the ironical object of writing. Gaining the reader's sympathy for one's characters, good ones and bad ones, as perhaps Dickens does, and George Eliot, Tolstoy, D. H. Lawrence and Joseph Conrad do, is a better way to write. It's braver, and riskier to sympathise with the nasty, to turn away from the easy target. 'Truth can never be told so as to be understood, and not be believ'd.' – William Blake

Afterword

❖❖❖❖❖❖❖❖❖❖❖❖❖❖

This Afterword was delivered by Nirad C. Chaudhuri on the celebrations for his 100th birthday in 1997; it has been included since it is both a fitting finale to the theme of this collection and to the work of a major literary presence. Chaudhuri's erudite, eclectic, provocative works were stimulated by his enquiries into the complex relationship between British culture and his root culture of India.

From: Nirad C Chaudhuri

Re: Centenary Celebration of Nirad C Chaudhuri on
          23 Nov 1997 at Trinity College, Oxford.

Mr Chairman and my lord, the Lord Lt. of Oxfordshire, Representative of the British Council, Ladies & Gentlemen,

You who are here to meet the centenarian Nirad C Chaudhuri, supposed to be a sprightly Robin Goodfellow with a partiality for pranks, must have been surprised to see a decrepit old man in an invalid chair. Such are the accidents of life. I myself am surprised and cannot understand how I have lived one hundred years. I find a hint or clue in some lines of Matthew Arnold, for it by recalling a few:

> *Thou hast not liv'd,*
> > *Why should'st thou perish, So?*
> *Thou hadst one aim, one business,*
> > *one desire . . .*
> *For early did'st thou leave the world, with powers*
> > *Fresh, undiverted to the world without,*
> *Firm to their mark, not spent on other things;*

But if that was the case, that too was not of my choosing. The Powers which had brought me into this world – and brought me weak unfit to survive – also gave me that compensation. I deserve no credit for it.

But in one respect I am exercising my will. My gratitude to you all is my own and created by my will. Please believe that.

I think I have said enough to show my gratitude to you.

So, Ave atque Vale

Hail and Farewell.

My admonition to myself has been, and to all others will be:

'Courage, yet more courage,

and always courage'

Thank you finally.

[Signed]

Nirad C. Chaudhuri

Biographical Notes

◆◆◆◆◆◆◆◆◆◆◆◆◆◆◆◆◆◆◆◆◆◆◆◆◆◆◆◆◆◆◆

Rukhsana Ahmad has written several plays for the stage and radio – even though her first love is fiction. She chose to translate Urdu poetry and fiction that especially moved or inspired her: *We Sinful Women* and Altaf Fatima's novel, *The One Who Did Not Ask*. Her novel *The Hope Chest* was published in 1996. Rukhsana is still working on her second novel, alongside her theatre and radio work.

Mulk Raj Anand, born in Peshawar in 1905 and currently living and writing in Mumbai, is a prolific novelist. His many works include *Coolie, Untouchable, Two Leaves and a Bud* and a trilogy: *The Village, Across the Black Waters* and *The Sword and the Sickle*.

James Berry has written and edited several books of poetry, and children's fiction. His poetry collections include *Fractured Circles, Lucy's Letters and Loving, Hot Earth Cold Earth* and *When I Dance*. As editor, his poetry anthologies include *Bluefoot Traveller* and *News for Babylon*.

Homi Bhabha's work has been included in a number of collections and anthologies, including *Questions of Third Cinema* and *Psychoanalysis and Cultural Theory: Thresholds*. The author of *The Location of Culture* and editor of the essay collection, *Nation and Narration*, Bhabha is currently working on *A Measure of Dwelling*, a theory of vernacular cosmopolitanism.

Nirad C. Chaudhuri was born in Bengal, India, in 1897; he settled in Britain in 1970, where he died in 1999 at the age of 101. His many works include *The Autobiography of an Unknown Indian, Passage to England, The Continent of Circe* and *Thy Hand, Great Anarch!* He wrote his last book, *Three Horsemen of the New Apocalypse* to coincide with his 100th birthday.

Ferdinand Dennis is the author of two travel books, *Behind the Frontlines: A Journey into Afro-Britain* and *Back to Africa*. His novels include *Duppy Conqueror, The Last Blues Dance* and *The Sleepless Summer*.

David Dabydeen, Professor of Caribbean Studies at Warwick University, has published numerous works of fiction, non-fiction and poetry. His latest novel is *Harlot's Progress*. His other novels include *The Intended* and *Disappearance*. His non-fiction includes *Hogarth's Blacks* and *Coolie Odyssey*.

G. V. Desani, born in Kenya in 1909, first came to Britain in 1926 for two years, as a seventeen-year-old, and then returned in 1939. He published his *chef d'oeuvre*, *All About Hatterr* in 1949. *Hali*, an extended prose poem, was first published in 1950. He has retired from his post of Professor of Philosophy in Texas.

Farrukh Dhondy is the author of many novels and short story collections, including *Bombay Duck, Black Swan* and *Janaky and the Giant*. Four of his plays have been staged in London theatres and several on television. He was formerly Commissioning Editor, Multicultural Programming, for Channel 4 TV (1984–97), and is currently working on a life of C. J. R. James.

Buchi Emecheta has written scripts for television and an autobiography. Her novels include *Joys of Motherhood, Second Class Citizens, In the Ditch, The Bride Price* and *Kehinde*. They have been translated into fourteen languages.

John Figueroa, who died in Britain in 1999, was a regular contributor to the famous Caribbean literary journal of the 1950s, *Bim*. He edited several anthologies of poetry, including *Caribbean Voices: an Anthology of West Indian Poetry (Vols 1&2)*. His own poetry collections include *Blue Mountain Peak* and *The Chase*.

Beryl Gilroy, a retired school teacher and educational psychologist, has written numerous school texts, and essay and poetry collections. Her many works of fiction include *Frangipanni House, Steadman and Joanna, Inkle and Yarico* and *Gather the Faces*. Her autobiography, *Black Teacher*, is a classic of its kind.

Attia Hosain, who died in 1998 at the age of eighty-four, was a broadcaster and writer. Her collection of short stories *Phoenix Fled* and her novel, *Sunlight on a Broken Column*, first published in 1953 and 1961 respectively, were reprinted by Virago in their Modern Classics series in 1988.

E. A. Markham, Professor of Creative Writing at Sheffield Hallam University, has published six collections of poetry, two of short stories and a novel. He is also the editor of *Hinterland: The Bloodaxe Book of West Indian Poetry*, and *The Penguin Book of Caribbean Short Stories*.

Dom Moraes's first book of poems, *A Beginning*, published when he was nineteen in 1957, won the Hawthornden Prize. It has been followed by three more collections, *Poems*, *John Nobody* and *Bedlam and Others*. He has also written his autobiography and twenty prose books based often on his travels on assignment as a journalist.